N – Z

BY JANE ELLING HAAS

ILLUSTRATED BY CAROLYN BRAUN

CPH
SAINT LOUIS

Thanks to Debbie Davis, Myra Farrell, Susie Fritsche, and Wendy Schultz—Christian day school teacher-friends and God's blessings to me. I praise God for our ministry in which we share educational ideas, highlight joyous teaching moments, and lift each other up to the Lord's care.

Copyright © 1998 Concordia Publishing House
3558 S. Jefferson Avenue, St. Louis, MO 63118-3968
Manufactured in the United States of America

CONTENTS

Introduction 4

Celebrate **N**ature 6

Celebrate **O**fferings 11

Celebrate **P**rayer and **P**raise 15

Celebrate **Q**uietness 19

Celebrate **R**ighteousness 22

Celebrate **S**anctification 26

Celebrate **T**rinity 30

Celebrate **U**nity .34

Celebrate **V**ictories 38

Celebrate **W**ater .43

Celebrate ☧mas .47

Celebrate **Y**ellow 53

Celebrate **Z**ion 57

Patterns 61

INTRODUCTION

WHAT IS A CELEBRATION CENTER?

A celebration center is where one person or a group of people come together to do one or more activities related to a Bible lesson in celebration of God's grace.

This book of ideas is designed to help you make and use hands-on activities with children in grades 3 to 5. The ideas also work well in intergenerational settings where adults and children can work together. You may use these ideas in Sunday, midweek, or day school settings; in family night celebrations at church; and in home-schooling and family devotion settings.

WHAT YOU WILL FIND INSIDE

This book provides themes listed alphabetically for the *second half* of the alphabet. For each theme, you will find the following:

- Suggestions for Scripture readings
- Bible stories to learn
- Special Bible verses to read and remember
- Suggested books to read
- Activities and directions to help reinforce the Scripture focus
- Illustrations and suggested materials to help you set up and prepare for the center and its activities
- Directions for each activity and patterns when appropriate

FIVE REASONS TO USE CELEBRATION CENTERS

1. Celebration centers emphasize learning by doing, touching, and using the five senses.
2. Centers invite interaction among learners of various age levels and between students and leaders.
3. Centers provide a change of pace for learning experiences from a traditional classroom approach.
4. Celebration centers encourage learners of all ages to read the Bible, share Bible stories, and reinforce their learning through daily life applications.
5. Centers complement lessons by providing opportunity to expand activities, discover new facts and relationships, and make concrete life applications.

Six Ways to Use Celebration Centers

1. Set up celebration centers in day school classrooms as additional activities for students to complete as time and space allow.

2. Engage in celebration centers as a supplement to a home-school curriculum.

3. Use center ideas as a supplement to your regular Sunday morning educational program. Teachers might direct a "center" room during the first or last 30 minutes of Sunday school or midweek school for all ages, including adults. Activities can reinforce what learners hear during their regular lesson time.

4. Create learning centers on special Sundays of the church year, in various seasons, or at any time that you want to provide intergenerational activities.

5. Invite all ages to participate in learning activities together during school vacations and use one or more classrooms for designing celebration centers. Encourage people to bring friends and neighbors as a way of reaching more with the Gospel.

6. Make celebration centers at home to do together as families. Invite friends and neighbors. Use center ideas in "cell" Bible study groups.

How to Use This Book

Read through each center entirely. The center setup is only one of several possibilities for how to present the theme and activities. Make adjustments according to your setting. Keep in mind that the books listed in the **Books to Read** section are not the only ones available on the theme. If working with older children, you will want to include books and Bible story collections at their reading level.

As you review the activities, keep in mind that some are student-directed while others are leader-directed. Also some activities may be too simplistic or too difficult for your students. Use those activities you feel are appropriate. Add your own ideas to the list. Feel free to adapt activities to meet the ages or abilities of your children. Use your imagination to make learning a fun, exciting experience as you discover new things together. Celebration centers should *involve, interest,* and *inspire.* Celebration centers should be *faith community* celebrations.

In addition to choosing the activities, you will need to gather the necessary materials to complete the activities. Some general items are needed for all the centers. These would include basic writing or craft supplies such as ruled paper, pencils, marking pens, construction paper, glue, tape, crayons, etc. You may need to provide items such as homemade play dough or items you normally keep in storage—such as tempera paint—to complete specific activities. Highlight which activities you want to do with your children as you read through the center. Then list the supplies you will need or the special arrangements you will need to make (for example, paint smocks, table coverings, or extra adult supervision). You may want to ask students, families, and friends to donate the items or to volunteer time to help complete the various activities.

CELEBRATE NATURE

SCRIPTURE TO READ:

Genesis 1:1–2:25; Psalm 96; 148; Proverbs 27:18; Jeremiah 17:7–8; Matthew 12:33

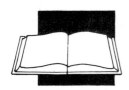

BIBLE STORIES TO LEARN:

God Makes the World (Genesis 1:1–2:3); God Made and Loves People (Genesis 1:26–2:25); God Rescues Adam and Eve (Genesis 3:1–24)

BOOKS TO READ ABOUT NATURE:

The Story of Creation (CPH, 59–1496); *The World God Made* (CPH, 59–1114); *God's Good Creation* (CPH, 59–1463); *Animals and Me ABC* (CPH, 56–1840); *The Fall into Sin* (CPH, 56–1486); *The Desert Critter Friends series* (CPH)

GOD'S WORD TO REMEMBER:

God saw all that He had made, and it was very good. *Genesis 1:31*

The earth is the LORD's, and everything in it, the world, and all who live in it; for He founded it upon the seas and established it upon the waters. *Psalm 24:1–2*

SET UP YOUR CENTER

Cut huge bubble letters from colorful poster board to spell **NATURE**. On each letter, glue nature items such as leaves, twigs, small pebbles, feathers, dried flowers, nutshells, seashells, cornhusks, pinecones, and popcorn and other seeds. Add stickers and magazine pictures that show other natural objects such as birds, insects, animals, trees, clouds, and plants. Attach the letters to a bulletin board, a wall, or a free-standing divider. Or use fishing line to hang the letters from the ceiling.

Write the following activities on individual note cards and place the cards inside a separate file folder or box. Place the folders or boxes near the **Nature** sign. Gather the materials necessary for the activities you selected. Place them in storage containers in the center.

ACTIVITIES

BIRDING

To the teacher: To prepare for this activity, place several books about birds from your library in the center. Look for books with colorful illustrations, such as *All the Birds of North America* (Jack L. Griggs, HarperPerennial, 1997). You might consider placing several pairs of small, inexpensive, low-power binoculars in a shoe box.

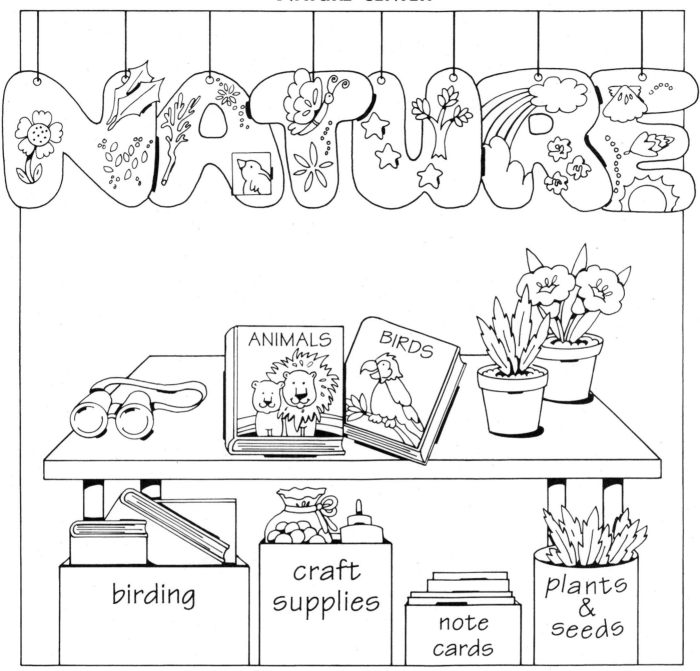

Can you identify the birds that live around your school? Look out a window or sit quietly on the playground and watch for different birds. Draw and color the birds you see. Compare your pictures with those in a bird book. Write the common name for each bird under the picture you drew. Make your own bird book using these drawings.

BUILD A BETTER BIRDHOUSE

Use wooden craft sticks and carpenter's glue to make a bird feeder or birdhouse of your own design. You might use other building supplies such as scraps of plywood or cedar, a hammer and nails, or tree bark. Ask for an adult's help if you use these items.

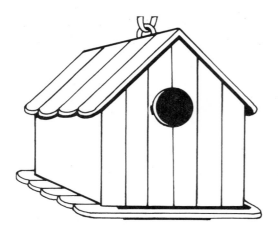

BUTTERFLY HOUSE

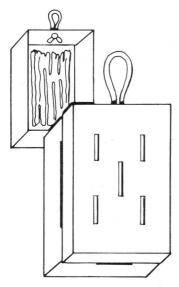

Line the inside bottom of a shoe box with pine bark. Make sure you use pine bark and not cedar bark. Cut several 2" slits in the box lid. Each slit should be about ½" wide. Tape the lid on the box. The slits will be large enough for a butterfly to squeeze through and cling to the cool, safe bark inside.

BUTTERFLY NET

Shape two wire hangers into a tube or egg shape. Cut the leg off a pair of pantyhose. Stretch the pantyhose leg over the wire frame, leaving one end open. Place a pine twig inside the tube for a butterfly to use as a perch.

NATURE NOTE CARDS

Cut 8½" × 11" sheets of construction paper in half. Fold the smaller pieces in half. Glue dried or silk flowers and greenery to the front. Make sure the petals and leaves lie as flat as possible. Place a sheet

of waxed paper over the flowers and pile several heavy books on top. Let dry. Use marking pens to add a favorite Bible verse or saying about God's creation. Use the stationery yourself or give it as a gift.

Trust in the Lord with all your heart...

NATURE PLACE MATS

Glue dried or silk flowers and greenery, stickers, and pictures of nature scenes cut from magazines to an 11" × 17" sheet of construction paper. Cover with a sheet of waxed paper and pile several heavy books on top. Let dry. Use marking pens to write a favorite Bible verse or a table prayer on the place mat. Cover with clear adhesive for durability.

Dear God, Thank You for our food. Amen

Dear God, this food is a blessing from You! Help me be a blessing to others too! Amen.

YUMMY DIRT SNACK

To the teacher: To prepare for the following activity, gather the necessary ingredients. Cover a work table with a vinyl tablecloth. Invite an adult or two to help supervise the children as they prepare the snack.

Spoon chocolate instant pudding into a small plastic cup. Add candy Gummi worms and insects as you fill the container. Crush chocolate sandwich cookies and sprinkle the crumbs as "dirt" on top of the pudding. Cut a drinking straw in half. Attach green construction paper leaves and colorful flower stickers or flower pictures cut from magazines to the straw halves to make flowers. Stick the flowers in the snack. Thank God for beautiful flowers and earthworms.

BIRDSEED SQUIGGLES

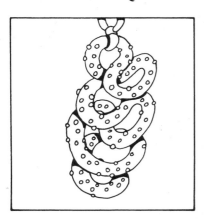

Squeeze a squiggly design of white glue onto a sheet of waxed paper. Sprinkle birdseed over the design. Make sure all the glue is covered. Let dry. Gently shake any loose birdseed into a container. Slowly peel the waxed paper away from the hardened glue. Tie a length of string or yarn to the top and hang the squiggle from a tree branch. Place the extra birdseed in a feeder.

FRUIT AND VEGGIE PRINTS

To the teacher: Precut apples, oranges, lemons, carrots, green peppers, potatoes, and any other "firm" food. Corncobs make interesting prints.

Insert a cob holder in each end for easy printing. Pour tempera paint into pie pans or vinyl-coated paper plates.

Spread the paint evenly over the bottom of the plate with a paintbrush. Press the cut side of the fruit or veggie into the paint, lift it, then press it onto construction paper. Lift it carefully to see your instant print! Use the paper as gift wrap or frame it for display.

You also can decorate paper lunch bags and wrapping paper with nature prints. Also try printing with twigs, leaves, walnut shells, rocks, seashells, and other firm items.

BERRY INK

Long ago, people wrote with stick pens they dipped into ink made from crushed berries. Make berry ink by placing ripe blueberries, blackberries, or strawberries into a small jar. Use a spoon to crush them to a pulp. Add a small amount of water and stir the mixture well. Place a paper towel over a cup, lightly pushing the towel into the cup. The paper towel will act as a strainer. Slowly pour the berry mixture through the towel into the cup. When the liquid has drained through the towel, throw away the towel and berry pulp. Pour the berry "ink" back into the jar.

To write or draw, dip a small twig with a pointy end into the berry ink. Make someone special a berry ink birthday card and add nature drawings or dried flowers.

COLORED CELERY TREE

This project demonstrates how a tree gets its water from the soil. Cut off the bottom of a celery stalk. Beginning at the bottom, use a knife to slice the stalk in two, ending halfway up the stalk. Fill two glasses ¾ full of water. Add food coloring to the water to make a different color in each glass. Mix well with a spoon. Place the two glasses next to each other. Slip one end of the celery stalk into each glass. Let set overnight. In the morning, the food coloring will have traveled up the celery stalk and the leaves will be beautiful colors!

LEAF RUBBINGS

Collect leaves from several different trees or bushes. Squeeze glue onto the sides of the leaves without raised veins and stick them on a sheet of paper. When dry, place a sheet of white drawing paper over the leaves. Remove the paper from a crayon and rub over the surface of the paper with the side of the crayon. The veins and shape of the leaf will appear. Change colors for each leaf.

LEAF SPONGE STENCILING

Place a small amount of acrylic, water-based craft paint in a pie plate or a vinyl-coated paper plate. Place a leaf on a sheet of heavy paper. Dip one end of a damp sponge in the paint, evenly coating the sponge's surface. Use your fingers to keep the leaf in one place on the paper. Dab the painted side of the sponge around the edges of the leaf, overlapping onto the paper. When finished, carefully lift the leaf to reveal the stenciled design.

NATURE ALBUM

Cut out pictures of nature items (leaves, plants, trees, animals, mountains, oceans, flowers, etc.) from magazines. Glue each picture or sets of similar pictures to a sheet of construction paper. Write a caption for each page. Add a simple prayer of thanks to God for each item. Assemble the pages into a book.

OBSERVE ARBOR DAY

Plant a new tree each year. Plant it on the school grounds or at a nearby park. The National Arbor Day Society provides free trees upon request.

ADOPT A TREE

Choose a tree near your school. Find out what kind of tree it is, read all about its species, and estimate how old it is. Write a story about your tree. Tell who may have planted it and all about its life history. Tie a special ribbon around your tree and thank God for trees.

CELEBRATE OFFERINGS

SCRIPTURE TO READ:

Genesis 4:3–5; 22:1–18; Leviticus 27:30; Psalm 116:17; Mark 12:33; Ephesians 5:1–2; Philippians 4:18–19; Hebrews 11:4

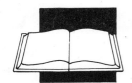

BIBLE STORIES TO LEARN:

The Offerings of Cain and Abel (Genesis 4:3–5); Abraham's Test (Genesis 22:1–18); God's People Bring Offerings for the Tabernacle (Exodus 25:1–8; 35:4–29); Wise Men Worship Jesus (Matthew 2:1–12); Jesus Feeds the 5,000 (John 6:1–13); The Widow's Offering (Luke 21:1–4); Jesus Died for Our Sins (Matthew 27:45–54)

BOOKS TO READ ABOUT OFFERINGS:

Abraham's Big Test (CPH, 59–1502); *Three Presents for Baby Jesus* (CPH, 59–1497); *The Visit of the Wise Men* (CPH, 59–1439); *What's for Lunch?* (59–1510); *The Boy Who Gave His Lunch Away* (CPH, 59–1138); *Jesus' Big Picnic* (CPH, 59–1472); *The Day Jesus Died* (CPH, 59–1516); *Good Friday* (CPH, 59–1451)

GOD'S WORD TO REMEMBER:

Through Jesus, therefore, let us continually offer to God a sacrifice of praise—the fruit of lips that confess His name. And do not forget to do good and to share with others, for with such sacrifices God is pleased. *Hebrews 13:15–16*

SET UP YOUR CENTER

Decorate a wall or bulletin board with colorful paper hands and feet, large paper money (bills and coins) cut from green and white construction paper, happy faces, and singing faces. Scatter red and pink hearts cut from construction paper around the bulletin board. Add the title **Hearts, Hands, Feet—My Offerings for Jesus.** Place recycling containers for newspaper, plastic, and aluminum cans in the center. Place folders and boxes containing the following activities on a small table near the bulletin board. Gather the necessary supplies for the activities you choose and place them in a storage unit in the center.

ACTIVITIES

WHAT DO I HAVE TO OFFER?

Look up the word *offering* in a dictionary. Write what it means in your own

words. An offering doesn't have to be *monetary* (giving money). Now look up the word *sacrifice*. How is an offering like a sacrifice?

Draw a picture of yourself or tape your photo to a sheet of paper. Write about the offerings you can give to God, to your family members, to friends and neighbors, and to others around you. See how quickly your "offerings" add up! Keep your offering list where you can see it every day. Ask God to help you offer these things out of love for Him and for others.

COIN BANK

Use a Pringle's can with a lid, margarine tub with a lid, or a film canister with a lid to make a coin bank. Ask an adult to cut a slit in the lid. Decorate the canister or box with symbols made from construction paper, marking pens, paint,

stickers, felt or fabric scraps, or whatever other materials you have on hand. Symbols could include a cross, praying hands, an offering plate, or an altar. Use this bank to hold your offering for God.

"I'm God's Child" Papier-Mâché Bank

To the teacher: To prepare for this activity, mix powdered papier-mâché from a craft store or use the following recipe. (Make a little at a time. It's hard to save.)

Papier-mâché Recipe: Pour ½ cup flour into a bowl. Add ½ cup water and stir. Paste should be the consistency of whipping cream before it's whipped (not thick pudding). Add water if paste is too thick.

Cut newspaper into 1″ wide strips. Blow up a round balloon. Lay one newspaper strip into the papier-mâché mixture at a time. Take it out of the mixture and brush off the excess (don't wad the paper and squeeze). Wrap the newspaper strip around the balloon. Add strips until the balloon is covered. Let this first layer dry overnight. Add a second and third layer, letting each layer dry completely. When completely dry, cut a slit about 3″ long and about ½″ wide in the top. Pop the balloon and remove the pieces of balloon by shaking it lightly. Throw away all the balloon pieces.

Use marking pens and yarn to make a self-portrait on a small paper plate. Glue it to the front of your balloon bank. Add arms and legs cut from construction paper. Use acrylic paint to add clothes to your bank.

Remember that God has made you His child, and He has blessed you with faith and with everything you need to live. As you place coins in your bank, say a thank-You prayer to God and name your blessings. Ask Jesus to help you offer your talents and gifts to serve Him.

Offering Basket

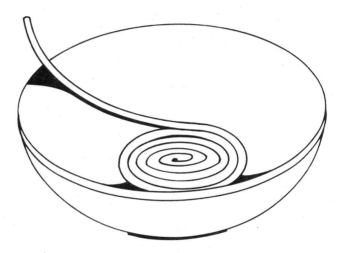

The Huichol *(WEE-chol)* Indians of Northwest Mexico make beautiful yarn paintings. The brilliant colors and interesting designs of these paintings tell stories about the history and religion of Native Americans. The Huichol make yarn paintings by pressing yarn into warm beeswax.

Use the Huichol art technique to make an offering basket. Cover the inside bottom of a Styrofoam or paper bowl with glue. Starting in the center of the bowl, wrap a length of colorful yarn in a circular pattern, using a craft stick to pat the yarn into the glue. Add more glue and start another color of yarn, continuing all the way to the top. When you reach the rim, flip the bowl over and glue yarn in a circular pattern to the outside bottom of the bowl. Continue until you reach the rim. Cut two lengths of yarn and glue a cross to the inside bottom of the bowl. Add crosses or other Christian symbols to the inside and outside of the bowl. Glue one continuous length of yarn around the rim of the bowl to finish. Let dry completely.

MY OFFERINGS FOR JESUS BOOKLET

Draw pictures of yourself doing things for others or using your talents to help others. Ideas for pictures might include reading to a younger brother or sister, picking up your clothes, or getting the mail for a neighbor. Write captions for each picture. Assemble the pictures into a book. Make a cover with the title **My Offerings for Jesus.**

SPECIAL MINISTRY PROJECTS

Jesus tells His people, "Love one another as I have loved you." You can give money, time, or talents to a special project. Look around your church, school, community, and neighborhood for ideas or use one of these suggestions.

1. Offer to help an elderly neighbor clean the house, mow or rake the yard, or run errands. Perhaps your family can help wash windows or winterize a home for someone who is unable to do the work.

2. Plant spring bulbs around your school or church grounds. Or ask your mayor if there is a planting project you could do at a park or other community property.

3. Sponsor a child through a not-for-profit agency. Ask your pastor or principal for suggested organizations.

4. Collect money for a special project or scholarship fund at your school. A project might include buying Bibles or Bible storybooks for each classroom or purchasing Christian artwork for each classroom.

5. Sponsor a collection for a crisis pregnancy center in your area. You can collect layette items, canned food, money, or pledges of volunteer time.

6. Recycle aluminum cans, newspapers, plastic containers, and clothing.

7. Recycle leftover Christian education materials. Organizations such as Concordia Gospel Outreach (1-800-325-3040) can help you send unused lesson material to people who really need it.

8. Decorate note cards with colorful illustrations and Gospel messages. Plan a field trip to share these cards and Jesus' love with residents of nursing homes or assisted care facilities.

9. Collect new school supplies and make back-to-school kits. Include a note that wishes the girl or boy a happy school year! Ask your principal or teacher to make sure the kits get to kids who need them.

CELEBRATE PRAYER AND PRAISE

SCRIPTURE TO READ:

Psalm 63:4; 113:2; Romans 12:12; 1 Thessalonians 5:16–18; James 5:13

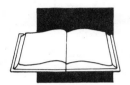

BIBLE STORIES TO LEARN:

Miriam Praises God (Exodus 15:1–21); Hannah Prays for a Son (1 Samuel 1:1–2:11); God Hears His People's Prayers (1 Kings 18:16–19:18; 2 Kings 18:1–20:11); Jonah Prays (Jonah 2:1–10); Mary Praises God (Luke 1:46–55); Simeon and Anna Welcome the Savior (Luke 2:21–38); Jesus Teaches Us to Pray (Matthew 6:5–15); Jesus Prays in Gethsemane (Luke 22:39–46)

BOOKS TO READ ABOUT PRAYER AND PRAISE:

Prayer: Learning How to Talk to God (CPH, 56–1395); *Sand and Shells, Carousels, and Silver Bells* (CPH, 56–1830); *God, I've Gotta Talk to You* (CPH, 59–1301); *God, I've Gotta Talk to You Again* (CPH, 59–1315); *Jonah and the Very Big Fish* (CPH, 59–1514); *The Man Caught by a Fish* (CPH, 59–1136); *Jonah's Fishy Adventure* (CPH, 59–1470); *Mary's Christmas Story* (CPH, 59–1499); *Mary's Story* (CPH, 59–1140); *The Lord's Prayer* (CPH, 59–1459)

GOD'S WORD TO REMEMBER:

I will praise You as long as I live. *Psalm 63:4*

Be joyful always; pray continually. *1 Thessalonians 5:16–17*

SET UP YOUR CENTER

Hang a picture of Jesus on the wall. If possible, use a picture of Jesus praying. In the worship area, place an empty cross, a Bible, an offering basket marked **Prayer Basket**, and a basket or container with the necessary supplies for the activities. Also include a container of rhythm instruments, several praise video- and audiocassettes, children's books about prayer, simple songbooks, and the pocket chart described in a following activity. Near the worship area, place large pillows and carpet squares for the children to use as they pray to and praise God.

ACTIVITIES

WHAT IS A PRAYER?

Read Jesus' prayers in the Bible. Did you know that some of the psalms are prayers too? Read Psalm 23, 46, 100, and 130. A prayer sounds like two friends talking: One friend is listening; one is talking. Who is the listener and who is the talker in each prayer you read in the Bible? Who is the listener and who is the talker when you pray? List ways that you can pray (for example, by talking or thinking). Write a

prayer to God as if you were sitting and talking to Him. Use it the next time you pray.

PRAYER BASKET

For whom would you like to pray? For whom would you ask others to pray? Print the names of these people on separate note cards and place them in the prayer basket in the worship area. Include a short sentence that explains why each person needs prayer.

Each day, take a card from the prayer basket. Pray for the person listed. You might use a pillow or carpet square to get comfortable as you talk with your heavenly Father. Put the card back after you're done praying so another person can pray for the individual too.

GOD'S ANSWERS TO PRAYERS

Has God answered a prayer you've listed on a prayer card in a way that you can see? Sometimes God answers no and sometimes He says to wait. Find that card in the basket and print God's answer on the card. Use marking pens to decorate the front of the note card or to draw a picture of God's answer. Each week, plan a special praise celebration to thank God for answering prayer. Sing "Praise God from Whom All Blessings Flow" and wave colorful scarves or streamers.

PRAYER POCKET CHART

To the teacher: Make a pocket chart by gluing envelopes or library card pockets to a sheet of poster board. Title it **Prayer Chart.**

Use marking pens to write prayer requests on note cards. Place the cards in a pocket on the Prayer Chart. When you have free time during the day, take several of the prayer requests, get comfortable, and talk with God. Put the cards back in the pocket chart when you finish praying. Remind your friends to pray too!

PRAYING PARTNERS

Decorate a tissue box and title it **Praying Partners.** Print your name on a slip of paper and put it inside the box. Ask your friends to do the same. Every Friday, draw a name out of the box. Pray for that person for the next week. You can tell the person you're praying for him or her or keep it a secret. You might want to leave notes that give clues to your identity and remind your partner that you are praying for him or her.

MY PRAYER LIST

Use markers or acrylic paint to decorate a ceramic, plaster of paris, wooden, or resin shape such as a heart, hand, or cross. Write **My Prayer List** on the shape. Attach a magnetic strip to the back. Cut construction paper into 3" wide strips. List names of people and events that need your prayers. Use the magnet to hang your prayer list on the refrigerator or a metal cabinet at home to remind you of who needs your prayers.

As God answers your prayers, write those answers that you can see beside each name or event. Praise God for always listening and answering.

PRAYER PILLOWCASE

Use fabric paint to decorate a plain pillowcase with your name, Christian symbols, and the names of your family members and friends. Let the paint dry completely. When you use the pillowcase, you'll have a reminder to pray.

PRAYER CAP

Use marking pens, fabric paint, glitter paint, or favorite pins to decorate a plain cap or a painter's cap. Place prayer reminders on your cap and wear it when you pray.

PRAYER SHIRT

Use fabric paint to turn a plain T-shirt into a prayer shirt. List special needs or people you want to pray for on the shirt. Wear your prayer shirt as you pray.

PRAYER SHOELACES

Use red, green, and blue fabric paint in tubes with fine points to draw hearts and crosses on white shoelaces. When the paint has dried, use the laces as a reminder to pray at all times.

PRAYER REMINDERS

Use a sheet of poster board and marking pens to make a prayer reminder. Print the acronym **ACTS** down the left side of the poster board. Fill in the explanation as listed below. Hang the prayer reminder in your bedroom or on the refrigerator to remind your whole family to pray.

A = Adoration (Tell God how wonderful He is.)

C = Confession (Tell God your sins and how sorry you are.)

T = Thanksgiving (Tell God thanks for everything He gives you.)

S = Supplication (Tell God what you need.)

PRAYER BRACELET

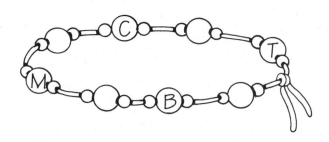

Make a unique bracelet by threading beads onto an elastic cord. Tie the cord in a slipknot to fit your wrist comfortably. Choose beads with bright colors or beads with letters. Suggested designs include threading beads with the first letter of each family member's name or threading beads of different colors to represent people and things for whom you want to remember to pray. Wear your bracelet as a reminder to pray throughout the day. Make a bracelet for a friend too!

PRAYER AND PRAISE WALL HANGING

To the teacher: To complete this activity, take the squares made by the children and connect them into a patchwork wall hanging. Add a casing at the top to insert a dowel rod so the hanging can be displayed. Or connect the squares, add a border around the squares, cotton batting, and a backing. Use a large-eye needle and lengths of yarn to tie the corners of each square. Hang the prayer and praise wall hanging in your worship area as a reminder that God loves to hear your prayers and praises to Him.

Use fabric paint to illustrate prayer and praise on a 12" square of light-colored cotton. You could show yourself praying or singing praises, or draw how you feel when you pray or praise God. Write your name or put your initials on the square.

CELEBRATE QUIETNESS

SCRIPTURE TO READ:

Psalm 23:1–2; Isaiah 32:17;
1 Thessalonians 4:11;
1 Timothy 2:1–2; 1 Peter 3:4

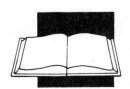

BIBLE STORIES TO LEARN:

Jesus Is Born (Luke 2:1–20); Jesus Teaches Us to Pray (Matthew 5:5–15); Jesus Prays in Gethsemane (Luke 22:39–46); Jesus Rises from the Dead (Mark 16:1–8; Luke 24:1–12)

BOOKS TO READ ABOUT QUIETNESS:

Baby Jesus Is Born (CPH, 59–1467); *The Shepherd's Christmas* (CPH, 59–1513); *Baby Jesus, Prince of Peace* (CPH, 59–1471); *The Lord's Prayer* (CPH, 59–1459); *The Story of the Empty Tomb* (CPH, 59–1517); *My Happy Easter Book* (CPH, 59–1493); *The Easter Women* (CPH, 59–1431)

GOD'S WORD TO REMEMBER:

[God] will quiet you with His love. *Zephaniah 3:17*

SET UP YOUR CENTER

Set aside part of the classroom as a Sound Center. If desired, place two refrigerator boxes together as a "sound room."

Make a poster or computer banner that reads **Quiet or Loud?** Place boxes of quiet games and quiet activities on a small table. Hang a full-length mirror near the center. Set up a tape- or CD-player for children to use. Have tapes of sounds and books. Gather the necessary supplies for the activities and put them in a storage container in the center.

ACTIVITIES

QUIET TIMES

Write a large, colorful Q on a sheet of poster board. Cut out pictures from magazines of people enjoying quiet times. Glue the pictures around the letter Q. Use marking pens to add your own descriptions of quiet times you enjoy.

PLAY DOUGH

What things are very quiet in our world? Use play dough to make quiet things. Ask a friend to guess what you made.

DOT TO DOT

Use a black marking pen to draw a picture of a quiet person or thing. Make it simple, such as a tree, a window, or your grandma. Put a sheet of tracing paper over your drawing. Use the black marking pen to make bold dots that outline your design. Choose a starting point and number each dot. Give the dot-to-dot activity to a friend to complete.

ANIMALS AND THEIR SOUNDS

Cut out pictures from magazines of animals that are quiet. Glue the pictures to sheets of construction paper. Write a short description of the animal and the sounds it makes. Put the individual pages together into a book. Punch holes and lace the pages together with yarn. Or put the animal pictures into a photo album. Make a second book of animals that are loud.

QUIET PUPPETS

Make a Quiet Quentin or Quiet Queen puppet. Use craft glue to add felt ears, eyes (or wiggly craft eyes), and a mouth to the toe of a thick sock. Remember that your quiet puppet always speaks gently and quietly.

NATURE COLLAGE

There are many quiet objects in the world God created. Make a collage of quiet things such as seashells; leaves; pressed flowers; feathers; pictures of butterflies, insects, the sun, and the moon; star stickers; and more. You can glue the objects to a sheet of poster board or put them in a shadow box.

DISCOVER SOUNDS

To the teacher: To prepare for this activity, place objects in margarine tubs, potato chip cans, and other unbreakable containers with lids. Label each container with a number. Objects might include beans, rice, cotton balls, ball bearings, nuts and bolts, pebbles, paper clips, cereal, strips of paper, facial tissue, clothespins, pencils and pens, etc.

Work with a partner to discover soft and loud sounds. Shake each container and guess what's inside. Don't peek! After you've written down all your answers, see how many you got right. How did your partner do?

I HEAR YOU!

To the teacher: To prepare for this activity, collect tapes or CDs with sounds.

Listen to the different tapes or CDs of sounds. Guess who or what is making each sound. Make your own tape of sounds. Tape different people speaking, singing, giggling, whispering, and praying. Ask a friend to guess whose voice it is. Are the sounds quiet or loud?

FOLLOW THE LEADER

Play this traditional game as a *quiet* game by taking off your shoes and playing in your socks. Lead others in motions that do not make a sound.

BIBLE PEOPLE CHARADES

Act out scenes from the Bible without speaking. How do you act out "loud" scenes—like the walls of Jericho falling—without making any noise?

MIRROR IMAGES

Ask a friend to play this quiet game with you. Stand in front of the mirror. Make a funny face or stand a certain way. How closely can your friend mimic you? Mimic your friend too. Try not to laugh.

QUIET FUN WITH CARDS

Play quiet card games such as "Find the Pair," "Go Fish," and "Crazy Eights."

QUIET READING TIME TOGETHER

Get comfortable and read quietly by yourself or with a partner. Take turns reading by paragraphs or by chapters.

CELEBRATE RIGHTEOUSNESS

SCRIPTURE TO READ:

Isaiah 42:6; Jeremiah 23:6; Hosea 2:19; Matthew 6:33; Romans 1:16–18; 4:3; 1 Corinthians 1:30; 2 Corinthians 9:9; 1 Peter 2:24

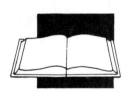

BIBLE STORIES TO LEARN:

God Rescues Adam and Eve (Genesis 3:1–24); Cain and Abel (Genesis 4:3–16); Noah and His Family (Genesis 6:9–9:17); Jacob Meets Esau (Genesis 33:1–16); Joseph Feeds His Family (Genesis 42:1–45:15); Jesus' Death and Resurrection (Luke 23:1–24:12); Philip and the Ethiopian (Acts 8:26–40)

BOOKS TO READ ABOUT RIGHTEOUSNESS:

The Fall into Sin (CPH, 59–1486); *Noah's 2-by-2 Adventure* (CPH, 59–1511); *The Story of Noah's Ark* (CPH, 59–1110); *Noah and God's Promises* (CPH, 59–1294); *Noah's Floating Zoo* (CPH, 59–1464); *Joseph Forgives His Brothers* (CPH, 59–1494); *The Day Jesus Died* (CPH, 59–1516); *Good Friday* (CPH, 59–1451); *The Story of the Empty Tomb* (CPH, 59–1517); *The Easter Women* (CPH, 59–1431)

GOD'S WORD TO REMEMBER:

He Himself bore our sins … so that we might die to sins and live for righteousness. *1 Peter 2:24*

Put on the new self, created to be like God in true righteousness and holiness. *Ephesians 4:24*

SET UP YOUR CENTER

Use butcher paper to make a large, chunky cross. Hang it on a wall or bulletin board. Or you can build a cross from blocks or similar-sized boxes. Cover the sides with paper. Tape a picture of Jesus to the cross. Title the cross **Right with God**. Gather the materials you will need to complete the selected activities. Place them in a storage unit in the center.

ACTIVITIES

RIGHTEOUSNESS LANGUAGE

Write your own definition for the word *righteousness*. If you're going to be righteous, you've got to be right—*all* the time! Is it all right to be half-right sometimes? Or one-third right? Or three-quarters right? Being partly right isn't good! You can't be half-right or half-happy or half-healthy. Either you are *all right* or you aren't righteous.

Read Romans 3:10, 20–22. We are separated from God because we are sinners. We cannot come to God on our own.

Because of His great love for us, God did something to remove the wall of sin that separated us from Him. He made us "right with God" by sending someone to do something so important that it was a life and death matter. Who did God send to make us right with Him?

Glue your photo or a self-portrait to the cross. When you see your picture, remember that because of what Jesus did for you on the cross, you are no longer separated from God. Jesus tore down the wall and made you "righteous" in God's sight! Use a red crayon or marking pen to add a heart near your photo.

Sin and Forgiveness Visual

To the teacher: To prepare for this activity, fill several spray bottles with water.

Using a seamstress marker, write the word *sin* in large letters on a piece of cotton fabric. Think about how Jesus died on the cross in your place so He could buy you back from sin, death, and the devil. He made you "righteous in God's sight." Spray the word *sin* with water. What happened? Thank Jesus for taking away *all* of your sins. Ask Him to help you keep from repeating your sins. Now take a green permanent marking pen and draw a large cross on your piece of fabric. Keep it as a reminder that Jesus has given you new life as a forgiven child of God.

Righteousness Poster Prayer

R
I love Jesus
G
Heavenly home
To save me
E
On the cross
U
S
N
Eternal life
S
Salvation!

Print the word *righteousness* down the left side of a sheet of poster board. Think of a phrase, sentence, or prayer that reminds you of the righteousness Jesus has won for you and begins with each letter in the word. Write them after the letters. Hang the poster in your bedroom to remind you of the wonderful things Jesus has done for you.

A Righteousness Demonstration

To the teacher: Supervise students as they perform this experiment. The hot water and detergent almost completely remove the stain while the other methods do not.

Spread ketchup on three different pieces of white fabric. Place one in a container of cool water. Place one in a container of cool water mixed with detergent. Place the third in a container of hot water mixed with detergent. Place a lid tightly on each container. Shake each one. What happens?

Two of the pieces of fabric remain stained. Sin *stains.* Sin hurts us and others. One sin leads to others. Sin spreads, gets deeper, and becomes impossible to get rid of by ourselves. One piece of fabric is clean. Jesus took the stain of sin away from us forever. He made us "white as snow"—righteous—in God's sight!

BIBLE WORDS REVIEW

Place a sheet of waxed paper over a sheet of white paper. Use a sharp pen or pencil to write a Bible verse about righteousness, such as Romans 3:22, on the waxed paper. Press hard as you write. Throw away the waxed paper. Exchange the white sheet of paper with a partner. Lightly rub the lead of a pencil over the paper and watch the Bible verse appear. Take turns reading what you have printed as Bible reminders.

CELEBRATION CROSS

To the teacher: To prepare for this activity, pop at least six quarts of popcorn. Remove all the unpopped kernels. Melt one stick of margarine and one large bag of mini-marshmallows together. Add the popcorn and two cups of gumdrops and/or jelly beans. Grease your hands well and press the popcorn and candy mixture into the shape of a large cross on a piece of waxed paper. Or make individual crosses for each child.

The cross is more than a symbol of suffering. It's also a sign of victory, a reason to celebrate. Jesus won the victory over sin, death, and the devil when He died and rose again. As you enjoy eating the celebration cross, remember that Jesus has made you righteous in God's sight.

BAPTISMAL SHELL

Use glitter paint to draw a cross in the center of a seashell (the clam-shaped shells work best) as a reminder of God's grace through Baptism. Add your name and baptismal date. You also can use self-hardening clay to make the shell shapes.

RIGHTEOUS ROBES

Cut head- and armholes in the end seam and the side seams of a large white pillowcase. Decorate your "righteous" robe with fabric paint, glitter paint, or fabric marking pens. Add baptismal symbols and pictures that remind you of your faith. Include butterflies—which represent new life—crosses, flowers, and happy faces. Add Bible passages that remind you that Jesus has made you righteous in God's sight.

CELEBRATE SANCTIFICATION

SCRIPTURE TO READ:

John 17:17–19; Acts 26:18; Romans 15:16; 1 Corinthians 1:2; 6:11; 1 Thessalonians 4:3; 5:23; 1 Peter 1:2

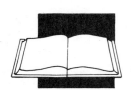

BIBLE STORIES TO LEARN:

Joseph Forgives His Brothers (Genesis 42:1–45:28; 50:15–21); Esther Helps Her People (The Book of Esther); Jesus Helps Us Love and Forgive One Another (Matthew 18:21–35; Mark 10:13–16); God Sends the Holy Spirit (Acts 2:1–47); Paul Proclaims the Gospel (Acts 17:1–34; 23:12–35)

BOOKS TO READ ABOUT SANCTIFICATION:

Joseph Forgives His Brothers (CPH, 59–1494); *The Queen Who Saved Her People* (CPH, 59–1194); *Jesus Blesses the Children* (CPH, 59–1500); *The Day the Little Children Came* (CPH, 59–1210); *Jesus and the Little Children* (CPH, 59–1481); *The Coming of the Holy Spirit* (CPH, 59–1452); *Peter and the Biggest Birthday* (CPH, 59–1480); *Somebody Lives Inside: The Holy Spirit* (CPH, 56–1557)

GOD'S WORD TO REMEMBER:

You were washed, you were sanctified, you were justified in the name of the Lord Jesus Christ and by the Spirit of our God. *1 Corinthians 6:11*

SET UP YOUR CENTER

Cut one large donut shape from sheets of dark purple, white, and green poster board. On each shape, print one of the following phrases: Holy Sinner (purple shape), Holy Jesus (white shape), Holy Spirit (green shape). Hang the three donut shapes side by side from the ceiling. Place a table under or near the shapes. Place containers with the necessary supplies for the activities on the table.

To introduce the center, explain that, as sinners, we are dark with sin. The dark purple color reminds us that we are born sinful and sin every day. But Jesus took our sins to the cross and washed us clean. The white color reminds us that His saving action "justified" us and made us righteous in God's sight. The green color reminds us that the Holy Spirit helps us grow in Christ Jesus. Think of how a plant grows strong and tall when it is given sunshine and water. God gives us everything we need to be His people—His holy, forgiven people—living a sanctified life by the power of the Holy Spirit.

ACTIVITIES

LANGUAGE OF SANCTIFICATION

Write your own definition for the word *sanctification*. To help you get started, remember that the Latin word *sanctus* means "holy." How does knowing the meaning of the root word help you figure out the meaning of *sanctification* and *sanctify*?

Think of something in your house that you use almost every day. When you wash your hair, you blow it dry. Your hair dryer has a special purpose—drying your hair. List other items you use every day for a specific job.

Did you know God has set you aside for a special purpose? He has sanctified you and made you holy through Jesus' blood. The Holy Spirit lives inside of you. God has done something very special for you. How did He do it? Read John 17:17 to find out how God sanctifies you.

SANCTIFICATION CHAIN STORY

Ask several friends to help you write a chain story. A chain story is one in which every person adds a sentence. This story will be about how God helps you and uses you as His holy people. One person starts the story by completing one of these sentences: "One bright, sunny day, I …" or "One dark, stormy night, I …" Write the action on a strip of paper. Staple it into a loop. The next person writes another portion of the story on a strip of paper and links it to the first and so on. Remember to focus on God's actions in your life as He sanctifies and keeps you in His Word and faith through the work of the Holy Spirit.

WALKING PUPPETS

Cut out large triangles from construction paper or poster board. At the bottom of the triangle, cut out holes large enough to stick your fingers through. Your fingers will serve as legs. Use marking pens or crayons to decorate the triangles to look like people. Take turns putting on puppet shows that show and tell a "sanctification story." How might these people show others the love of Jesus that the Holy Spirit gives them?

STYROFOAM STENCILS

Make "holy people." Trace or draw the outline of a cookie-cutter person on a clean Styrofoam meat tray. Cut it out. Draw a heart in the center of the person. Use the tip of the scissors to push through the tray along the outline of the heart until it comes out. Brush a thin coat of tempera paint over the shape of the person and press it, painted side down, onto a sheet of white paper. Your person will appear as a pretty color with a white heart inside.

Display this at home as a reminder that Jesus has saved you from your dirty sins and the Holy Spirit lives in you, making you God's holy (sanctified) person. (You can use the stencil to make a "God makes you holy" greeting card for someone special.)

"HOLY ME" MASK

Cut out eyeholes from a large paper plate. Glue or tape a craft stick or a paint stick to the back of the plate to serve as a holder. Draw or decorate the paper plate to show how happy you are because the Holy Spirit lives in your heart and makes you God's holy child.

PERSONAL BANNER

Cut a piece of felt or other sturdy fabric to serve as a banner background. At the top, fold 2" of fabric down and cut short slits into the fabric (don't go through the top edge). Unfold the fabric and weave a dowel rod through the slits to serve as a hanger. Attach letters that spell out your favorite Bible verse as well as Christian symbols cut from fabric or felt. Or use fabric paint, glitter paint, or fabric marking pens to add these to your background. Tie colorful ribbons to the ends of the dowel rod. Hang your banner as a reminder that the Holy Spirit keeps you holy each day so you can serve a special purpose in God's kingdom.

SOAP PAINTING

Use a pencil or nail to draw a simple Christian symbol on a new bar of soap. Use a design that reminds you that the Holy Spirit lives in you. It could be a heart, cross, dove, butterfly, flower, crown, or smiling face. Press hard enough to make a deep impression in the soap. After you've completed your design, use the tip of a paintbrush or a cotton swab dipped in a small amount of acrylic paint to fill in the design. Add lettering with a fine-point marking pen. Let dry. Give the soap bar to someone special as a reminder that the Holy Spirit lives in him or her too.

SEEDS OF FAITH

Plant bean, marigold, or grass seeds in small planters of potting soil. Cut sheets of construction paper to fit around the planters. Decorate the paper with words and Christian symbols that remind you of God's love and care for you each day. For example, you might use the phrases: "Because Jesus lives, I will live too." "The Spirit will guide you into all truth." "I live by faith. I grow with the Holy Spirit's help." Give the plants to people who need to hear how much Jesus loves them.

SANCTIFICATION TOTEM POLE

Use a marking pen to divide a paper towel tube into four or five sections. In the first section, draw and color a dove or make the triangle symbol for the Holy Trinity. In the second section, draw a picture of yourself. In the remaining sections, draw pictures of times when the Holy Spirit helps you act in a Christ-like way around your family, friends, or neighbors. Show things you could do or say to share Jesus' love. When complete, make sturdy paper tabs to glue the pole to a cardboard base. Display your work of art and use it to tell others how the Holy Spirit is at work in your life.

CELEBRATE THE TRINITY

SCRIPTURE TO READ:

Deuteronomy 6:4; Psalm 2:7; Matthew 3:13–17; 28:19; 2 Corinthians 13:14; Galatians 4:6

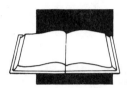

BIBLE STORIES TO LEARN:

John Baptizes Jesus (Matthew 3:13–17)

BOOKS TO READ ABOUT THE TRINITY:

The Story of Creation (CPH, 59–1496); *The World God Made* (CPH, 59–1114); *God's Good Creation* (CPH, 59–1463); *Baby Jesus Is Born* (CPH, 59–1467); *God Promised Us a Savior* (CPH, 59–1442); *Baby Jesus, Prince of Peace* (CPH, 59–1471); *The Story of Jesus' Baptism and Temptation* (CPH, 59–1503); *The Coming of the Holy Spirit* (CPH, 59–1452); *Peter and the Biggest Birthday* (CPH, 59–1480); *Somebody Lives Inside: The Holy Spirit* (CPH, 56–1557); *3 in 1* (CPH, 56–1314)

GOD'S WORD TO REMEMBER:

Go and make disciples of all nations, baptizing them in the name of the Father and of the Son and of the Holy Spirit. *Matthew 28:19*

SET UP YOUR CENTER

In a corner of your room, place a large box with three large paper bags inside it. With brightly colored paint or marking pens, label the large box **Trinity—Three-in-One.** Label one of each of the paper bags as **Father, Son,** and **Holy Spirit.**

Write each activity on a separate note card. Place the note cards inside the paper bags. It doesn't matter which activity is inside which bag or that children mix the activities as they return them to a bag. This will add to the concept of three persons in one. Collect the necessary items to complete the projects you selected. Place them in a storage unit in the center.

ACTIVITIES

TRINITY LANGUAGE

Tri is a root word that means "three." The word *trinity* means "three-in-one." Another name for the Trinity is "Triune God." *Triune* means "three-one." Three and one, both at the same time! God is Triune!

Read the Apostles' Creed. We believe that God our Father created us and that He takes care of us. We believe that God the Son—Jesus—was born to be our Savior and King. He died for us on the cross to win us forgiveness. His resurrection gives us the promise of living with Him in heaven when we die. We believe that God the Holy Spirit is a gift in our lives. He

lives in our hearts and helps our faith to grow strong. The Holy Spirit sanctifies us and helps us say and do Christ-like things.

Separate a sheet of construction paper into three columns. Put one of the following at the top of each column: **God the Father, God the Son, God the Holy Spirit.** Write the things that each member of the Trinity does under the appropriate heading. Refer to the Apostles' Creed, look at hymns or songs that talk about the Trinity, or look up Bible references that talk about each person. Don't forget to list the names we use to identify each person in the Trinity.

TRINITY SYMBOLS

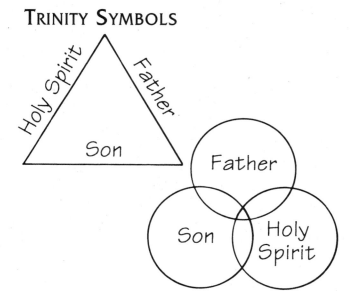

The most common symbol used to show the Trinity is a triangle with equal sides. This is called an equilateral triangle. Draw one or cut out an equilateral triangle from construction paper. There are three sides of the triangle and three members of the Trinity. Print the name for one member of our Triune God along each side: **Father, Son,** and **Holy Spirit.**

Another common symbol for the Trinity is three circles of the same size linked together. The separate circles show that the Father is not the Son nor the Holy Spirit, the Son is not the Holy Spirit nor the Father, and the Holy Spirit is not the Father nor the Son. When we see where the circles connect, we remember that together they are one God—the Father is God, the Son is God, and the Holy Spirit is God!

Design and draw your own diagram or symbol that shows the three persons in the Triune God. You might use paper, paint, or even a computer to complete this project.

STAR MOBILE

Make a star ornament to remind you that God's best gift, Jesus, was born for all people and died and rose again to win forgiveness and eternal life for us. Cut drinking straws into five 6" pieces. Tie the straws together with red embroidery floss or single-ply yarn. Tie a loop hanger to the top. On a slip of paper, write a thank-You prayer to God for sending Jesus. Tie it to the star.

You can make a Trinity symbol by tying three stars together with yarn to make a simple mobile.

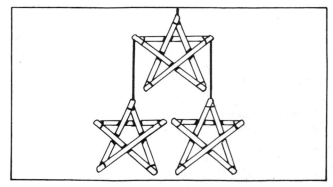

WORD RUBBINGS

Write names of God or words that are associated with the Trinity on sheets of poster board. (You might use Triune, Trinity, Three-in-One, Father, Son, Holy Spirit, Maker, Heavenly Father, Creator, Redeemer, Savior, Sanctifier, Spirit of God, Comforter.) Trace each word with a thick line of white glue. Let dry. Place a sheet of white paper over the words. Gently rub the unwrapped side of a dark crayon over the letters. Watch your words appear on the paper! Tell a friend what these words mean to you. Display your poster as a reminder of your one true God.

SANCTUARY SYMBOLS

Walk through your church sanctuary. Look at the symbols in the worship area. Draw the things you see that remind you of the Holy Trinity. Which symbols remind you of God the Father, of God the Son, and of God the Holy Spirit?

TRINITY MURAL

Hang a large sheet of butcher paper on a wall. Use bold lines to divide the paper into three equal sections. Label each section with the name of one member of the Triune God: **Father, Son, Holy Spirit.** Paint pictures in each section that remind you of the work of the Father, Son, and Holy Spirit. For example, draw pictures of things that God the Father created, of Jesus on the cross, and of a baptism.

TRINITY MOSAIC

To the teacher: Provide a 6"-square sanded wooden base for each student to construct a mosaic. Provide different materials to use to design a symbol for the Trinity, such as seashells, smooth or colored stones, pieces of vinyl or other sturdy fabric, chenille wires, wooden or ceramic beads, thick yarn, buttons, or tissue paper.

Draw a Trinity design on paper. Then transfer the design to the wooden base. Glue items to the base that will outline or fill in the design. Ask an adult to add two or three coats of clear shellac in a well-ventilated area, allowing each coat to dry completely. Display the Trinity mosaic as a reminder of the Father, Son, and Holy Spirit—our Triune God.

PLANTER BOX

Use scraps of wood to build a planter box. You'll need five pieces of wood that are the same size. Sand them smooth. Have an adult help you use a glue gun or a hammer and nails to put the boards together to make the planter. Use acrylic paint to decorate the sides of the box with favorite symbols of the Holy Trinity. When the paint is dry, dip a soft cloth in brown shoe polish and gently rub over the wood to make it look stained. Ask an adult to spray the box with clear acrylic spray in a well-ventilated area.

Add soil and plant seedlings or tulip bulbs. Water your plants as needed and place the box in a warm, sunny window. As you enjoy the plants, remember the work of God the Father (Creator), God the Son (Redeemer), and God the Holy Spirit (Sanctifier).

PLANTER POT

Use acrylic paint to decorate a clay pot with favorite symbols of the Trinity. Use a permanent marker to write **Father, Son,** and **Holy Spirit** or a favorite Bible verse on the pot. When the paint is completely dry, ask an adult to spray it with clear acrylic spray in a well-ventilated area.

Add soil and marigold or bean seeds. Water your plants as needed and place the pot in a warm, sunny window. As you enjoy the plants, remember the work of God the Father (Creator), God the Son (Redeemer), and God the Holy Spirit (Sanctifier).

THE DOXOLOGY

The words of the common doxology, "Praise God from Whom All Blessings Flow," were written by Thomas Ken, who lived from 1637 to 1711. He survived a horrible fire in London that destroyed 80 percent of the city. Then he suffered through the horrors of a plague that killed thousands of people. In every hardship, Bishop Ken praised and thanked God. It's also said that when a lookout on the Mayflower sighted land after 67 days, the passengers and crew dropped to their knees and sang the doxology.

Write your own words to the melody of the doxology. Include people and things for whom you praise God. Sing your new doxology with a friend or share it with your class to sing together.

CELEBRATE UNITY

SCRIPTURE TO READ:

2 Chronicles 30:12; Psalm 133; Romans 15:5–6; Ephesians 4:1–6; 11–13; Philippians 2:1–5; Colossians 3:12–14

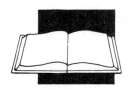

BIBLE STORIES TO LEARN:

God Made and Loves People (Genesis 1:26–2:24); God Saves Noah and His Family (Genesis 6:1–9:17); Joseph Forgives His Brothers (Genesis 42:1–45:15; 50:15–21); God Gives Victory at Jericho (Joshua 6:1–25); Jesus Changes Water into Wine (John 2:1–11); Jesus Helps Peter Catch Fish (Luke 5:1–11); Jesus Walks on the Water (Matthew 14:22–33); God Sends the Holy Spirit (Acts 2:1–47)

BOOKS TO READ ABOUT UNITY:

3 in 1 (CPH, 56-1314); *The Story of Creation* (CPH, 59–1496); *The World God Made* (CPH, 59–1114); *God's Good Creation* (CPH, 59–1463); *Noah's 2-by-2 Adventure* (CPH, 59–1511); *The Story of Noah's Ark* (CPH, 59–1110); *Noah's Floating Zoo* (CPH, 59–1464); *Joseph Forgives His Brothers* (CPH, 59–1494); *The Fall of Jericho* (CPH, 59–1473); *Jesus' First Miracle* (CPH, 59–1445); *Jesus Walks on the Water* (CPH, 59–1474); *The Coming of the Holy Spirit* (CPH, 59–1452); *Peter and the Biggest Birthday* (CPH, 59–1480)

GOD'S WORD TO REMEMBER:

May the God who gives endurance and encouragement give you a spirit of unity among yourselves as you follow Christ Jesus, so that with one heart and mouth you may glorify the God and Father of our Lord Jesus Christ. *Romans 15:5–6*

SET UP YOUR CENTER

Cut a large heart from red poster board. Cut lips, hands, and footprints from white paper. Glue the shapes onto one side of the heart. On the opposite side, glue white letters to spell *unity.* Hang the heart so both sides can be seen. Place the items for the activities in storage containers near the heart.

ACTIVITIES

OUR TRIUNE GOD

Almost every word that begins with *uni* means that the person, place, or thing has something to do with the concept of "one" or "oneness." We believe that God the Father, God the Son, and God the Holy Spirit are one God. We call the Three Persons our TriUNE God. Look up *triune* in a Bible dictionary. Write your own definition for this special word. Share it with a friend.

SEVEN THINGS THAT ARE ONE

Read what the apostle Paul wrote when he wanted to tell the people of Ephesus that God gives the gift of unity to all believers (Ephesians 4:4–6). Cut out seven large hearts from construction paper. Tie them together with yarn to form a mobile. On each heart, use glitter pens to write a key word or phrase from Paul's message. You'll find seven things that are one in his message! (Here's a hint: one body, one Spirit.) When the Holy Spirit helps us apply these to our lives, we are all UNIted in faith.

PRAYERS FOR UNITY

Write simple prayers for unity—for a happy Christian family, for power from the Holy Spirit, for Jesus' love and forgiveness, for more people to believe in Jesus as their Savior, for peace and unity in the world. Write each prayer on a separate index card. Put the cards in a box or basket. Pull out one prayer card each day to use during class or individual prayer time.

Uni Things

Look up the prefix *uni* in a dictionary. What does it mean? On a sheet of poster board or construction paper, make a UNI Chart that lists words that begin with the prefix *uni*. Here's a few words to get you started: the UNIted States, UNIcorn, a military UNIt, and a choir singing in UNIson.

FINGER PUPPETS

Snip the fingers off cotton work gloves. Use the finger sections to make finger puppets. Use fine-point marking pens to draw a face on each fingertip. Glue yarn

to the fingers for hair, cotton for beards, and fabric scraps for clothes. Make puppets that look like friends, family members, store clerks, bank tellers, mail carriers, firefighters, doctors, and police officers.

Work with a friend to write a short skit that tells how important it is to work together to accomplish a goal. Tell how God has provided everything we need, including forgiveness through His Son, Jesus. Write a song about working together to conclude the skit. Use a favorite melody.

PING-PONG VOLLEYBALL

To the teacher: To play this game, you'll need a ping-pong table or a large table. Divide the class into two equal teams. Line up each team on opposite sides of the table. Put a ping-pong ball in the middle of the table.

At the signal, everyone blows toward the ball. The goal is to score a point by blowing the ball off the opposite side of the table. It takes unity for a team to accomplish this!

BUBBLE BASKETBALL

To the teacher: Make a bubble mixture by combining 6 cups water, 2 cups Joy dishwashing liquid, and ¾ cup corn syrup (to give bubbles extra strength). Make the bubble mixture at least four hours before use. Provide commercial bubble wands or stretch out wire coat hangers. Leave part of the hanger as a handle. Wrap tape around any sharp edges. Use this mixture outside.

In groups of three or four, make a monster bubble and work together to blow it across the school grounds. It will take a lot of UNIty to keep the bubble going up instead of down.

BALLOONY-BALL

To the teacher: To play this game, work together to move furniture into one area of the room. Tie yarn or string between the backs of two chairs and place this "net" in the center of the cleared space. Blow up a balloon. Divide players into two equal teams. To play this game outside, place a volleyball net between two posts in a sandy or grassy area. Each team uses a bedsheet to toss and catch a water-filled balloon.

Work together to keep the balloon in the air and to pass it back and forth over the "net."

A Community of Hearts

Cut a heart from construction paper. Use glitter pens, shapes cut from greeting cards, marking pens, or stickers to decorate both sides of the heart. Write your name on the heart. Punch a hole in the top of the heart. When everyone is finished, string all the hearts together as a garland to decorate the classroom. Add cross and dove shapes at different points on the garland to remind you that God—the Father, Son, and Holy Spirit—is at the center of your community of believers.

Community Praise Window

To the teacher: To prepare for this activity, cover a work area with a vinyl tablecloth or with layers of newspaper.

Make a stained-glass window. On a sheet of typing paper, outline a simple Christian symbol using a thick, black permanent marker. Outline the edge of the paper with the marker too. Color your picture with crayons. Pour a small amount of salad oil on a cotton ball. Use the cotton ball to spread the oil evenly over the back of your picture. When your picture is completely dry, hang it in a window. Or you and your friends can make one large stained-glass window by joining all your pictures together. The light that shines through your stained-glass window is a reminder that Jesus is the Light of the world.

Praise and Prayer Pockets

Use an 11" × 17" sheet of construction paper as a background. Glue three library card pockets or envelopes to the paper. Label them **Family, Helpers,** and **Friends.** Cut out pictures of community helpers from magazines. Glue the pictures of helpers, as well as photos of family members and friends, to index cards. Sort the picture cards into the correct pockets. Use your pocket chart to give you prayer ideas. (You could add a pocket for church workers and include pictures of your pastor, teachers, or missionaries.)

CELEBRATE VICTORIES

SCRIPTURE TO READ:

Psalm 20:5; 21:1, 5; 44:6–8; 60:12; 129:2; 1 Corinthians 15:54, 57; 1 John 5:4–5

BIBLE STORIES TO LEARN:

God Leads His People out of Egypt (Exodus 12:31–42; 13:17–15:21); God Gives Victory at Jericho (Joshua 6:1–25); God Uses Gideon to Save Israel (Judges 6:1–7:21); God Gives David Victory (1 Samuel 17:1–58; 2 Samuel 5:17–25); Jesus Shows His Power and Glory (Matthew 4:1–11; 8:23–27; 17:1–9); Jesus Enters Jerusalem (Matthew 21:1–11); Jesus Shows His Power over Death (Luke 24:1–12); 1 Corinthians 15:20–22)

BOOKS TO READ ABOUT VICTORIES:

Moses and the 10 Plagues (CPH, 59–1291); *Moses and the Freedom Flight* (CPH, 59–1478); *The Fall of Jericho* (CPH, 59–1473); *David and Goliath* (CPH, 59–1457); *The Boy with a Sling* (CPH, 59–1116); *David and the Dreadful Giant* (CPH, 59–1483); *The Story of Jesus' Baptism and Temptation* (CPH, 59–1503); *The Little Boat That Almost Sank* (CPH, 59–1111); *Jesus Calms the Storm* (CPH, 59–1468); *Jesus Stills the Storm* (CPH, 59–1462); *Jesus Enters Jerusalem* (CPH, 59–1455); *God's Easter Plan* (59-1461); *Jesus Is Alive* (CPH, 56–1626); *The Story of the Empty Tomb* (CPH, 59–1517)

GOD'S WORD TO REMEMBER:

With God we will gain the victory, and He will trample down our enemies.
Psalm 60:12

But thanks be to God! He gives us the victory through our Lord Jesus Christ.
1 Corinthians 15:57

SET UP YOUR CENTER

Place a table in a corner of your classroom. Cover it with a vinyl tablecloth. Set out containers holding a variety of non-perishable snacks (granola, trail mix, crackers and bagels, dried fruit, apples, bananas, cookies, nuts). Add utensils, paper plates, and napkins.

Explain that after we experience a victory (athletic, academic, or talent competition), we celebrate by inviting our friends to a victory feast. This will be the "feast table." Determine guidelines for allowing students to get snacks (for example, at certain times during the day, only after lunch, only when work has been completed).

Provide pre-cut poster board in pennant and banner shapes. Place containers of supplies under the table for the activities. Hang a VICTORY! banner (computer generated or handmade) behind or above the table.

ACTIVITIES

THE MEANING OF VICTORY

To experience a victory, we need to defeat an enemy—there has to be a struggle or a fight, a bad situation that needs to be overcome. Sin causes such problems—the sin that every person is born with and lives with every day. The victory Jesus won for us on the cross is victory over sin and the devil.

Some people know they are victorious. They believe Jesus won the biggest victory of all when He died and rose again—the victory over sin, death, and the devil. Some people don't know about Jesus' victory. They need to hear that message. What does the word *victory* mean to you? Write a short definition in your own words. List victorious people you know or about whom you have read.

39

VICTORY CARDS AND BADGES

List as many "victory" words as possible. Then use these words to make a card to tell someone how important Jesus' victory is. Or make "victory" badges that say **Jesus makes me victorious!**

VICTORY GARDEN

During World War II, U.S. citizens planted victory gardens. They grew their own vegetables for their meals and saved as much money as possible by going without luxuries. The money they saved they gave to military leaders to buy tires and gasoline for the troops.

Grow your own victory garden. Plant bean seeds in small planters. Tend the garden carefully and thank God for the many victories He gives you. If you have space outside, consider planting a real victory garden and donate the produce to a local food pantry or shelter.

VICTORY PENNANT

Choose a poster board pennant shape. Use colorful marking pens or tempera paint to design a victory pennant. It should show what God has done for you through Jesus Christ. What special words could you include about the victory? What designs or symbols could you use to show how Jesus has given you the victory?

VICTORY STORY

Write a short story about a victory in your life. The victory could be a spelling bee or a race you won or a sports team you played on that won. Or maybe God has helped you live with a physical challenge or a tough situation in your family and you're doing great. Include ways that show how God has given you the victory, including the greatest victory through Jesus. Share your story with a friend.

VICTORY WALK

To the teacher: To prepare for this activity, place a starting line about 15' from a finish line. Give each child two 12" square sheets of newspaper. At the end of the race, give each participant a wrapped candy or other small treat.

Line up along the starting line. At the signal, place the newspaper squares on the floor, one in front of the other. Then place one foot on each square. To move forward, step onto the first square, pick up the newspaper at the back, move it to the front, step onto it, and continue to the finish line.

It doesn't matter who finishes first or last, everyone is a victorious winner.

PACKED LIKE SARDINES

This is a reverse game of hide-and-seek. "It" hides alone. All other participants count to 30, then look for "It." As each player finds "It," he or she joins "It" in the hiding place. Soon the players are crowded into the hiding place like sardines. Everyone's a winner! "It" chooses the next person to hide.

VICTORY CIRCLE TOSS

Everyone stands in a circle. One person throws a beanbag or a foam ball to another and shouts "Victory!" The receiving person names someone in the Bible to whom God has given a victory or a time when God helped him or her defeat the devil. Then the person with the beanbag tosses it to another person and shouts "Victory!" The game continues until everyone has had at least one turn.

MOVING MOUTH PUPPETS

To the teacher: To prepare for this activity, photocopy the puppet pattern on page 61, one for each child.

Choose one victorious person from the Bible (for example, Joshua, Deborah, Gideon, David, Esther, Jesus, Paul). Cut out a puppet face. Fold along the dotted lines, accordion style, so the top and bottom lips touch. Add eyes, a nose, a mouth, and hair. Put craft glue on the

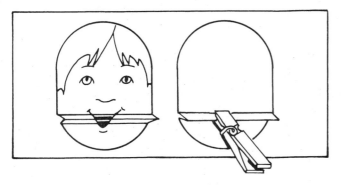

inside of the gripping section of a clip clothespin and "clip" the fold of the puppet. Let dry. Use your puppet to tell about the victories that God helped him or her win!

VICTORY WIND CHIMES

To the teacher: To prepare for this activity, make the following recipe.

Craft Dough Recipe: Mix 1 cup flour, ¼ cup salt, and 2 tablespoons powdered tempera paint (any color). Add ¼ to ½ cup water. If sticky, add more flour. Mix the dough well. Store it in a sealed bag. Make as many colors of dough as you wish. (You can use food coloring instead of tempera paint. Just add several drops to the water before you mix it into the dry ingredients.)

Use a rolling pin to roll the dough to about ⅜" thick. Use cookie cutters to cut out a variety of Christian symbols (crosses, fish, hearts, people). Use a toothpick or drinking straw to poke a hole in the top and bottom of each shape. Use a pencil or pen to write victory words or spell *victory* in the shapes. Place the shapes on a foil-covered cookie sheet and bake at 250° for one hour. Place cooled shapes on newspaper. Ask an adult to spray the shapes with acrylic sealer in a well-ventilated area. Let dry. Use yarn or heavy fishing line to hang these wind chimes from a tree branch or a thick dowel rod.

VICTORY WITNESS BALL

To the teacher: To prepare for this activity, collect a variety of small gifts (at least one for each child) such as stickers, wrapped candies, coins, crosses, hearts, small pictures of Jesus, Christian messages written on slips of paper, or tiny candles. Choose one of the gifts and wrap crepe paper around it. As you continue to wrap the crepe paper into a ball, insert other gift items at uneven intervals until you have wrapped all the gifts into a crepe paper ball. Glue the end of the crepe paper to the ball.

Ask everyone to sit in a circle. Pass the crepe paper ball to the person to your right. As he or she unwraps the ball and discovers the first gift, give one reason this person is special to you. Also share the Good News of Jesus' victory over sin, death, and the devil. As each gift is found, pass the ball to the next person. The person who passes the ball shares something special about the person doing the unwrapping. Continue around the circle until everyone has had a turn.

VICTORY PILLOWCASE

Design a picture or symbol for your pillowcase that reminds you of the victory Jesus has won for you. Place several layers of newspaper inside a white pillowcase. Use colorful crayons to draw the design on the pillowcase. Press firmly as you draw and color. Put a single layer of paper towels over your design. Ask an adult to iron gently over the paper towels until the wax from the crayons melts into the paper towels. Your picture will be permanently imprinted on your pillowcase! (Wash the pillowcase in warm water on gentle.)

As you say your prayers and get ready to sleep on your pillow, remember that Jesus loves you and has given you the victory over sin, death, and the devil.

CELEBRATE WATER

SCRIPTURE TO READ:

Genesis 6:1–9:17; Exodus 14:21–31; Psalm 1:3; 23:2; 42:1; Proverbs 25:21; Isaiah 12:3; 43:2; 49:10; Jeremiah 17:8; 31:9; The Book of Jonah; Matthew: 3:13–17; Mark 9:41; Luke 5:1–11; John 2:1–11; 13:1–17; 21:1–25; Acts 16:16–34; 27:1–28:6; Hebrews 10:22; 1 Peter 3:21; 1 John 5:6–8; Revelation 7:17; 21:6

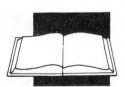

BIBLE STORIES TO LEARN:

God Saves Noah and His Family (Genesis 6:1–9:17); God Gives His People Water (Exodus 15:22–27, 17:1–6); God Sends Jonah to Preach His Word (The Book of Jonah); John Baptizes Jesus (Matthew 3:13–17); Jesus Changes Water into Wine (John 2:1–11); Jesus Helps Peter Catch Fish (Luke 5:1–11); Jesus Washes His Disciples' Feet (John 13:1–17); Jesus Appears at the Sea of Galilee (John 21:1–25); Paul and the Jailer at Philippi (Acts 16:16–34); God Saves Paul from a Shipwreck (Acts 27:1–28:6)

BOOKS TO READ ABOUT WATER:

Noah's 2-by-2 Adventure (CPH, 59–1511); *The Story of Noah's Ark* (CPH, 59–1110); *Noah's Floating Zoo* (CPH, 59–1464); *Jonah and the Very Big Fish* (CPH, 59–1514); *The Man Caught by a Fish* (CPH, 59–1136); *Jonah's Fishy Adventure* (CPH, 59–1470); *The Story of Jesus' Baptism and Temptation* (CPH, 59–1503); *Jesus' First Miracle* (CPH, 59–1445); *The Fishermen's Surprise* (CPH, 59–1139)

GOD'S WORD TO REMEMBER:

No one can enter the kingdom of God unless he is born of water and the Spirit. *John 3:5*

This water symbolizes baptism that now saves you … by the resurrection of Jesus Christ. *1 Peter 3:21*

This is the one who came by water and blood—Jesus Christ. … God has given us eternal life, and this life is in His Son. *1 John 5:6, 11*

SET UP YOUR CENTER

Make a water collage from magazine pictures or photos of water glued to a sheet of poster board. Hang the poster over a table. Cut out letters from varied shades of blue construction paper to spell **Water, Water Everywhere!** Attach the letters to a wall or bulletin board near the table.

Provide dishpans and plastic containers of various sizes, writing materials, an instant print camera and film, and craft supplies. Set these on and around the table. Collect the materials necessary to complete the projects you selected. Place them in a storage unit in the center.

ACTIVITIES

A WATER TABLE

To the teacher: To prepare for this activity, place a vinyl tablecloth on a table and set up a water center. Include dishpans of water, measuring utensils, plastic containers, seashells, etc. Provide vinyl aprons for students to wear.

As you experiment at the water center, remember that God makes you His child through the water of Baptism.

WATERSCAPE

To the teacher: To prepare for this activity, add equal parts of water and vegetable oil to a clean two-liter soda bottle. Add several drops of food coloring (any color). Screw the lid on tightly and wrap masking tape around it.

Shake the bottle. What happens? As you move the water back and forth in the bottle, tell a friend how Jesus calmed the storm (Matthew 8:23–27). Remember that God has all power over the water and the wind.

WATER INTO WINE

Read how Jesus changed water into wine (John 2:1–11). Practice telling the story out loud. Invite a friend to hear the story. Before the friend arrives, place seven clear plastic jars in front of you. Leave the first six jars empty. In the last jar, pour a

package of grape drink mix. When you describe how Jesus tells the servants to fill the clay jars, pour water into each container. When you describe how Jesus asked the servants to take a glass to the master to taste the wine, give your friend the seventh jar with the drink mix. Proclaim this is the best wine ever. Share how wonderful it is that Jesus loves us enough to take care of even everyday things like something good to drink.

RAIN SPATTER PAINTING

Let God's rain help you paint. First, use tempera paint to paint shapes on a sheet of white drawing paper. When it rains, place your painting on a sidewalk or other flat area outside. Leave it out in the rain for only a few seconds (if you leave it out too long, the rain will cause the paint to run too much). Let your painting dry

completely. See the different patterns the rain made. At the bottom of your painting, write a thank-You prayer to God for the rain.

SWEET POTATO PLANT

Plant a sweet potato in a glass of water. Push four or five toothpicks halfway into a sweet potato around the bottom third of the potato. Rest the toothpicks on the rim of a clear glass container so the bottom third of the potato is inside the container. Add water until it covers about an inch of the potato. Put the glass where it will get good sunlight. Keep the bottom inch of the potato in water.

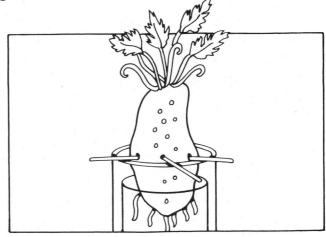

Watch the potato carefully for signs of growth. In a couple of weeks, roots will grow from the bottom and sides of the sweet potato. Then purple sprouts will grow from the top of the potato. The sprouts will turn into vines and green leaves will appear. Either leave the potato plant in the glass or plant it in a container of potting soil.

MAKE A TERRARIUM

A terrarium is a closed container in which plants or reptiles live in a controlled environment. Gather the following for this project: a large jar with a lid, pot-

ting soil, small leafy plants, small rocks, a hammer and nail, and water.

Wash the jar and remove any labels. Add potting soil. Plant the small plants. Add the rocks. Sprinkle enough water into the jar to wet the soil. Use the hammer and nail to hammer five to eight small holes in the lid. Screw on the lid tightly. The moisture the plants use from the soil will condense inside the jar so the plants will continually have water and produce oxygen.

PLANTS GROW BOTH WAYS

Watch a plant grow up and down. Fill a jar to the rim with water. Place a nylon net over the top of the jar so it just touches the water. Put two or three lima bean or green bean seeds on the net. Watch the roots develop and grow toward the water. Watch the leaves sprout and grow toward the light.

FISH OUT OF WATER

Many of Jesus' helpers had been fishermen before they left everything to follow Jesus. When Jesus said, "Come, follow Me," these fishermen became fishers of people. The Greek letters for the word *fish* are IXΘUS. These letters are also the first letters of the Greek words for "Jesus Christ, God's Son, Savior."

Cut fish shapes from sandpaper. Use a bright crayon to write IXΘUS on one side of the fish and your name on the other. Punch a hole in the mouth of each fish. Attach long lengths of yarn and hang the fish around the room. Or attach the fish to a large fishnet hung across the corner of the room. The next time you go fishing or you see fish in an aquarium, remember that Jesus helps *you* to be a fisher of people. He helps you tell others about His love for them.

Or place a sheet of white paper over the sandpaper fish shape. Remove paper from a crayon and rub the side of the crayon over the white paper. Display the fish etchings.

FISH SIGNS

Early Christians placed fish signs on their doors to let others know that a Christian family lived inside. Some people still do this today. When you are out with your family, count how many fish signs you see on car trunks, bumpers, or even at places you shop or homes you visit. Make a fish sign for your car or home.

WATER PLAY

Place a small wading pool full of water on a level area outside. Bring out a variety of objects. Experiment with the objects to see which sink and which float. Use balsa wood to make boats, then hold races. Fill small squirt guns and squirt water to write Gospel messages on a sidewalk. Use sponge shapes and paintbrushes to paint water decorations on a driveway. Water plants or trees.

Celebrate ☧mas (Christmas)

Scripture to Read:

Isaiah 9:2–7; Luke 1:26–2:20

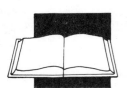

Bible Stories to Learn:

God Rescues Adam and Eve (Genesis 3:1–24); The Promise of the Savior Brings Joy (Zephaniah 3:14–20); An Angel Visits Mary (Luke 1:26–38); Jesus Is Born (Luke 2:1–20)

Books to Read about Christmas:

The Fall into Sin (CPH, 59–1486); *God Promised Us a Savior* (CPH, 59–1442); *Mary's Christmas Story* (CPH, 59–1499); *Mary's Story* (CPH, 59–1140); *Baby Jesus Is Born* (CPH, 59–1467); *My Merry Christmas Arch Book* (CPH, 59–1488); *Baby Jesus, Prince of Peace* (CPH, 59–1471)

God's Word to Remember:

A Savior has been born to you; He is Christ the Lord. *Luke 2:11*

Set Up Your Center

Use a bulletin board as a dimensional background for this center. Divide the bulletin board in half. On one side, use a green construction paper chain to make a Christmas tree. Place a gift box at the base of the tree. Inside the box, put a picture of Baby Jesus. The box lid should be removable. On the other side of the bulletin board, make a wood cross. Cut a crown from gold poster board or cover cardboard with gold foil wrapping paper. Place the crown on top of the cross. Title the bulletin board **JESUS—Our Savior and King**. Place supplies for the activities in file folders, cardboard boxes, and laundry baskets around the table.

Activities

God's Plan

When Adam and Eve ate the fruit of the tree in the middle of the Garden of Eden, they disobeyed God. They sinned. Because of their action, all people have been born with sin. We can't do anything to get rid of sin by ourselves. But God knew just what we needed. He promised a Savior for the world. He kept His promise when He sent His Son, Jesus, to earth.

Have you heard the phrase, "Jesus is the reason for the season"? Christians know that Jesus came to earth to take away our sins and make us right with God. God's Son, Jesus, grew up to suffer

Jesus—our Savior and King

Christmas games

luminarias supplies

gift-making items

merry music makers

and die for us on a cross. Then He came to life again and proclaimed victory over the devil, sin, and death. Jesus *is* the reason we celebrate and observe all seasons—Advent, Christmas, Lent, and Easter!

Use marking pens, paint, or colored pencils to draw pictures that show God's plan for the salvation of all people—Jesus' birth, His death, and His resurrection. You might make one picture that shows all three events, separate pictures of each event, work with friends to make a mural, or make greeting cards that depict the Good News of salvation. Share your pictures with those who need to know the salvation we have because of Jesus.

CHRISTMAS SEASON FACTS

Make a trivia game about Christmas. Cut index cards in half. Print a question about Christmas on one side and the answer on the other. Use a Bible,

Christmas books, magazines, and encyclopedias to help you find interesting facts about Christmas and Christmas traditions. Here are some questions and answers to get you started.

- What two Greek letters did early Christians use for Christ and which we sometimes use as a shortcut to write Christmas? (*Answer:* Chi and Rho. ✗ These are the letters that represent the first two sounds for the Greek word for Christ.)
- When did people first celebrate Jesus' birthday on December 25? (*Answer:* In the fourth century A.D., more than 300 years *after* Jesus was born.)
- Why did Christians choose December 25 to celebrate Christmas? (*Answer:* The Romans had chosen this day to worship the sun, which warms the earth and makes crops grow. Early Christians chose the day to worship Christ—the Son of God.)
- What does "December" mean in Latin? (*Answer:* It means tenth month, but it became the 12th month when the calendar was changed.)
- When was the celebration of Christmas forbidden? (*Answer:* In the 1600s.)
- Why was the celebration of Christmas forbidden? (*Answer:* The Puritans thought Christmas had become too worldly.)
- Was the celebration ever forbidden in the United States? (*Answer:* Yes. As late as 1870, American children in Puritan families went to school on Christmas.)
- When was Saint Nicholas born? (*Answer:* In the fourth century A.D.)
- Who was Saint Nicholas? (*Answer:* As a young boy, Nicholas was orphaned and inherited much money. Because he loved God and the poor, Nicholas used his wealth to help others. After the kind, generous man died, people honored "Saint Nicholas" on December 6.)

- Who wrote the Christmas carol "Silent Night"? (*Answer:* Father Joseph Mohr, a priest in an Austrian village. He lived in the early 1800s. He wrote the words after the church organ had broken down on Christmas Eve. Father Mohr and the church organist sang the words on Christmas Day to a newly composed tune.)
- What was another name people used for "Silent Night"? (*Answer:* People liked the carol so much they called it a "Song from Heaven.")

Here are some more questions. Can you find the answers to add to your trivia cards?

- Who began the tradition of decorating a tree for Christmas?
- Who wrote "Away in a Manger"?
- What does the word "advent" mean?
- How many candles are in an Advent wreath? What does each candle represent?
- Why do some people line their driveways and sidewalks with luminarias?
- Which Old Testament prophet spoke most often about the future birth of the Messiah?
- Why do people string popcorn and cranberries at Christmas?

MAKE LUMINARIAS

Luminarias is a Spanish word for "lanterns." You can make simple luminarias. Turn down the tops of white or brown paper lunch bags. In each bag, pour about 1" of sand or kitty litter. Place a votive candle in the sand in the center of each bag. On Christmas Eve or Christmas Night, line your driveway and sidewalk with the paper bags. Ask an adult to light the candles. Sing Christmas carols and welcome Jesus, the Light of the world.

TANGRAM PUZZLE

To the teacher: To prepare for this activity, photocopy the Tangram pattern on page 62 for each child.

The Tangram puzzle is a matching game invented thousands of years ago in Asia. You can arrange the shapes in abstract patterns or make your own pictures. First, use the pattern to cut the seven puzzle pieces from poster board. Then use the pieces to make a manger for baby Jesus, the stable, or a star. There are only two rules: You must use all seven pieces in any picture, and you cannot overlap any pieces.

SPOOL NATIVITY SET

Collect empty thread spools. Use fabric scraps, cotton balls, yarn or embroidery floss, large wooden beads, marking pens, craft glue, and chenille wires to make people for a Nativity scene. Glue a large wooden bead to the top of a spool for a head. Let dry. Then add facial features, cotton beards, yarn or floss hair, and fabric clothing. Make animals by placing the spools on their sides and adding chenille wire for feet and furry fabric pieces for hides.

EGG AND GOLD CHRISTMAS CARD

Paint an "egg and gold" masterpiece. (Look up Gentile da Fabriano in an encyclopedia to find out more about egg and gold painting.) Use a pencil to lightly sketch a Nativity scene or angel on a stiff sheet of paper. Paint your picture using "egg tempera." Make "egg tempera" by mixing egg yolk (save the egg whites) and tempera paint. Let the paint dry. Then paint the egg white where you want gold to be. Sprinkle the egg white with gold glitter. Let dry at least 15 minutes, then shake off the extra glitter.

I WITNESS T-SHIRTS

Design a simple illustration that shows the true meaning of Christmas. Draw the design directly on a T-shirt with dark crayons. Press firmly as you draw or color. When your design is finished, cover it with paper towels. Ask an adult to help you gently iron the design until the wax bleeds into the shirt. (It will take about 3 minutes.) To set the design into the fabric, wash the T-shirt in cold saltwater.

JEANS CARRYALL BAG

Recycle jeans that don't fit or are worn out into this carryall bag. Cut off the pant legs a few inches below the crotch. Fold the pants inside out. Use strong thread to sew straight across the bottom of each cutoff leg. Fold the pants right-side out. Cut rope or cord 12″ longer than the waist measurement of the pants. Thread the cord through the belt loops, then tie the cord ends together. On opposite sides of the bag, pull up on the cord to form handles. Use a longer length of cord if you want to carry the bag like a purse.

A Special Collection

Decorate a shoe box with wrapping paper or aluminum foil. Add pictures cut from magazines or old greeting cards. The pictures might be of the items your friend collects. Place items you know your friend doesn't have inside the box and present it as a thoughtful gift.

Fragrant Sachets

To the teacher: To prepare for this activity, cut fabric into 8″ squares. Fill spray bottles with water and fragrance mixtures. Provide cotton balls. You might offer fragrant extracts—such as lemon, orange, vanilla, peppermint, or strawberry—in addition to the fragrance mixtures.

Choose a fabric square. Spray a cotton ball with one of the fragrance mixtures or place a drop or two of an extract on the ball. Place the cotton ball in the center of the fabric square. Use a 12″ length of gift wrap ribbon or embroidery floss to tie the corners of the fabric together. Tie the ribbon into a loop or a bow. Place each sachet in a resealable bag to hold the fragrance until you can give it as a gift.

Photo Ornaments

To the teacher: To prepare for this activity, provide several photocopies of the ornament shapes on pages 63–64. Each child can select the shapes he or she wants to use to make the photo ornaments.

Glue or tape a small photo of yourself to the center of a holiday ornament shape cut from construction paper. On the opposite side, print the year and a favorite Bible verse. Ask an adult to help you cover the photo ornament with clear contact paper. Decorate your ornament with glitter, puff paint, or sequins. Punch a hole at the top and tie a narrow ribbon or cord through the hole to serve as a hanger.

Celebration Shakers

Put buttons, pebbles, coins, or rice into metal bandage boxes. Tape the boxes shut. Decorate with construction-paper cutouts or stickers. Put dried beans in large plastic egg containers. Tape the eggs shut and decorate with stickers. Use chenille wires or twist ties to fasten jingle bells to holes punched in margarine lids or plastic cups. Use all these celebration shakers to praise God as you sing Christmas carols and hymns.

STARS AND STREAMERS

Cut a large star from poster board. Cover it with aluminum foil. Use a gold glitter pen or gold paint to write your name on the star. Let dry. Cut long strips of crepe paper. Attach the paper streamers to the star's points. Wave your stars and streamers as you sing Christmas carols and move around the room together to music. Remember the angels' song in the heavenly sky on the night Jesus was born.

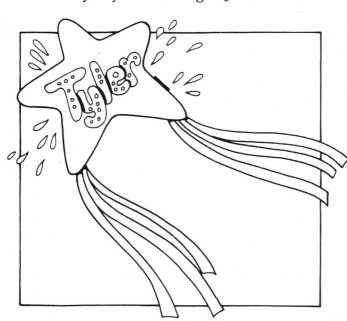

SONG POSTER

To the teacher: To prepare for this activity, have a tape recorder and a supply of blank tapes (one per child) in the center.

Make a giant Christmas card on poster board that features your favorite Christmas hymn or carol. Use bright marking pens to write the words to the song. Draw pictures on the poster to illustrate the song. Gather your friends to record the song on an audiocassette. Give a copy of the cassette and a song poster as a special gift.

BOTTLE BLOWERS

Fill eight empty soda bottles, all the same size, with different levels of water. Blow over the top of the bottles to hear musical notes. Adjust the water levels until you can play a scale. Try to play simple Christmas melodies such as "Away in a Manger" or "Silent Night."

Celebrate Yellow

Scripture to Read:

Genesis 1:3; Job 22:25;
Psalm 27:1; 84:11; 119:105;
Habakkuk 3:4; Malachi 4:2;
Matthew 5:14; 13:43; 17:2;
2 Corinthians 4:6; Ephesians 5:8;
2 Peter 1:19; 1 John 1:5

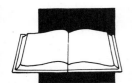

Bible Stories to Learn:

God Makes the World
(Genesis 1:1–2:3); Jacob
Dreams at Bethel (Genesis
28:10–17); An Angel Visits Mary (Luke
1:26–38); Jesus Promises His Light of
Life (John 8:12); Jesus Heals a Man
Born Blind (John 9:1–12); Jesus Shows
His Glory (Matthew 17:1–9); Jesus Rises
from the Dead (Luke 24:1–12); God
Sends the Holy Spirit (Acts 2:1–47);
Saul Becomes a Christian (Acts 9:1–20)

Books to Read About Yellow:

The Story of Creation (CPH,
59–1496); *The World God
Made* (CPH, 59–1114); *God's Good
Creation* (CPH, 59–1463); *Mary's
Christmas Story* (CPH, 59–1499); *Mary's
Story* (CPH, 59–1140); *Jesus and
Bartimaeus* (CPH, 59–1485); *The Story of
the Empty Tomb* (CPH, 59–1517); *My
Happy Easter Book* (CPH, 59–1493); *The
Easter Women* (CPH, 59–1431); *God's
Easter Plan* (CPH, 59–1461); *Jesus Is
Alive* (CPH, 56–1626); *The Coming of the
Holy Spirit* (CPH, 59–1452); *Peter and the
Biggest Birthday* (CPH, 59–1480)

God's Word to Remember:

The Lord is my light and my
salvation. *Psalm 27:1*

For God, who said, "Let light shine out
of darkness," made His light shine in
our hearts to give us the light of the
knowledge of the glory of God in the
face of Christ. *2 Corinthians 4:6*

Set Up Your Center

Hang yellow and white Christmas
lights in a corner of your room. You
might place the lights in the shape of a
candle and flame or in the shape of a
heart. Or you might spell the name *Jesus*
in bright lights.

Hang yellow balloons of various
shapes and sizes around the center. Add
yellow crepe paper, gold garland, or other
bright, light decorations. Place the necessary supplies for the activities in containers on a table.

Activities

Tie a Yellow Ribbon

To help you remember that Jesus is the
Light of the world, cut a length of yellow
ribbon. Tie it around your wrist as a
bracelet. Each time you look at the ribbon,
remember that Jesus died and rose for you
to take all the darkness of sin away.

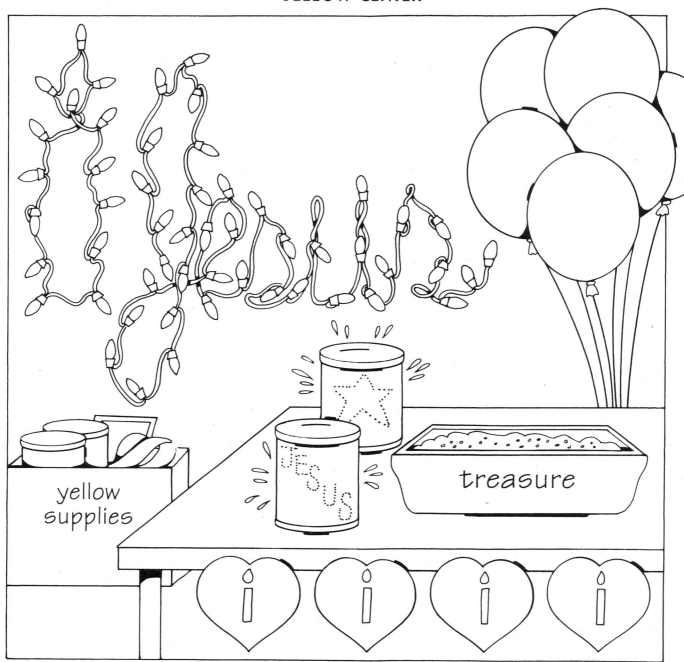

Tie yellow ribbons around your classroom doorknob, your bedroom doorknob, or around each of your family members' kitchen chairs as reminders of Jesus, our Light.

Cut short lengths of yellow ribbon and attach small gold safety pins. Give the yellow ribbons to friends to wear as you tell them, "Jesus is the Light of the world."

WRITE A SURPRISE MESSAGE

Cut large hearts from yellow construction paper. Use a yellow crayon to add designs or Bible verses about Jesus, our light. Press firmly as you draw and color. Paint over your heart with dark watercolor paint (black, violet, or blue). Surprise! Your yellow messages shine through! Make surprise messages to give to people who need to hear how much Jesus loves them.

LIGHT OF THE WORLD LANTERN

Fill metal coffee cans or large soup cans with water and freeze until solid. Cut a sheet of construction paper to fit around the can. Write **Jesus** on the paper and add a simple illustration, such as a candle or a sun. Attach the paper to the can with clothespins or paper clips.

Place the can on a thick, folded towel, in case the ice melts. Ask an adult to help you use a hammer and nail to punch holes through your paper pattern into the metal. When you finish punching along your design, punch two holes opposite each other at the top of the can. Throw away the ice.

Attach a wire handle. Put a votive candle inside the can. Place the lantern on a safe base (a ceramic tile floor or concrete). Ask an adult to light the candle. **NOTE:** Do not touch the handle while the candle is burning. (You can use a small flashlight instead of a candle.)

BRIGHT, YELLOW FLASHLIGHT

Use a gold glitter pen to write favorite Bible verses about Jesus' light and glory or about God's beautiful creation on the handle of a flashlight. Let dry. Cut a square of yellow cellophane. Use a rubber band to secure the cellophane to the lighted end of the flashlight. Now the flashlight will burn a bright yellow. Keep your flashlight by your bed as a reminder of Jesus, the Light God sent to the world.

YELLOW AND GOLD TREASURE HUNT

To the teacher: To prepare for this activity, place 20 to 30 pennies or other small yellow or gold objects at the bottom of a dishpan. (Objects could include measuring cups, funnels, birthday candles, keychains, yellow spoons, buttons, etc.) Pour enough yellow cornmeal into the container to cover the pennies or objects.

Wear a blindfold as you search through the cornmeal to locate the hidden treasures. As you find each object, try to identify it without removing the blindfold. To make the game more interesting, wear cotton or rubber gloves. How do the gloves change the feel of the objects as you search for them?

FEEL THE YELLOW

Make a "yellow feely bag" from a pillowcase or a large, stretchy sock. Place yellow and gold items inside the bag. Ask your friends to reach inside and guess the items by touch. Suggestions for yellow items include a scarf, plastic sunglasses, fabric, a stuffed animal, barrette, lump of play dough, cookie cutter, sheet of paper, pencil, lemon, or a plastic clothespin.

PLANT YELLOW FLOWERS

To the teacher: To prepare for this activity, set up a potting station. Cover a table with newspaper or a vinyl tablecloth. Provide Styrofoam cups, bags of potting soil, scoops or spoons, flower seeds, cotton gloves, and watering cans.

Plant flower seeds that will bloom with yellow flowers. Look for marigolds, petunias, nasturtiums, and pansies. Fill each cup ⅔ full of potting soil and add seeds. Sprinkle with water. Place the potted seeds in a warm, sunny window. Keep the soil moist.

Yellow Finger Paint

On a sheet of waxed paper, aluminum foil, glazed shelf paper, or a nonabsorbent commercial fingerpaint paper with a high gloss, place a few tablespoons of liquid starch. Sprinkle dry yellow tempera paint on the starch. Blend the mixture with your fingers.

Yellow Object Rubber Stamps

Cut tire inner tubes into 3" square pieces. Gather the tire pieces, sharp scissors, wooden spools or blocks of wood, rubber cement, and ink pads or tempera paint. Carefully cut shapes, numbers, words, or letters from the inner tube. Use rubber cement to glue the shape *backward* to a piece of wood or to a spool. Let dry.

Use your shape as a stamp. Press your stamp on a yellow ink pad or use a paintbrush to apply yellow tempera paint. Print your design on a paper bag, a sheet of construction paper, or a blank note card to make wrapping paper or stationery. You might make several stamps and start a collection of unique stamps.

Yellow Play Dough

To the teacher: To prepare for this activity, make this play dough recipe.

Play Dough Recipe: In a saucepan, mix 4 cups flour, 8 tablespoons cream of tartar, 2 cups salt, ½ cup salad oil, and 4 cups water. Cook over low heat. Remove from heat when the mixture forms a ball (about 3 to 5 minutes). Stir in yellow food coloring. Let cool. Knead the dough until all the ingredients are well-blended.

Or bring the following ingredients and let the children make their own play dough (you'll need enough for each child to participate). In a large bowl, mix 3 cups flour and ¼ teaspoon salt. Add yellow food coloring to 1 cup water. Add the water and 1 tablespoon oil to the flour mixture. Use your hands to mix the ingredients well. Add more flour or water if the dough is too sticky or too stiff.

Use the yellow play dough to make sunshine and candle shapes that remind you of God's Light to the world—Jesus.

CELEBRATE ZION

SCRIPTURE TO READ ABOUT ZION AND MOUNTAINS:

Psalm 2:6; 87:2; Isaiah 2:3; 28:16; 52:7–8; Jeremiah 50:5; Zechariah 9:9; Mark 9:2–9; Hebrews 12:22

BIBLE STORIES TO LEARN ABOUT ZION AND MOUNTAINS:

God Saves Noah and His Family (Genesis 6:1–9:17); Jesus Teaches the Beatitudes (Matthew 5:1–16); Jesus Feeds 5,000 People (Matthew 14:13–21); Jesus Feeds 4,000 People (Matthew 15:29–39); The Transfiguration (Matthew 17:1–9); Jesus Enters Jerusalem (Matthew 21:1–11); Jesus Promises to Take Us to Heaven (Matthew 25:31–46); The Ascension (Acts 1:1–11)

BOOKS TO READ ABOUT ZION AND MOUNTAINS:

Noah's 2-by-2 Adventure (CPH, 59–1511); *The Story of Noah's Ark* (CPH, 59–1110); *Noah and God's Promises* (CPH, 59–1294); *Noah's Floating Zoo* (CPH, 59–1464); *What's for Lunch?* (CPH, 59–1510); *The Boy Who Gave His Lunch Away* (CPH, 59–1138); *Jesus' Big Picnic* (CPH, 59–1472); *Jesus Enters Jerusalem* (CPH, 59–1455); *Jesus Returns to Heaven* (59–1476)

GOD'S WORD TO REMEMBER:

They will enter Zion with singing; everlasting joy will crown their heads. *Isaiah 51:11*

Come, let us go up to the mountain of the LORD. *Micah 4:2*

SET UP YOUR CENTER

Does your classroom lend itself to creating a learning center in a loft? Wherever you locate your Zion center, title it **Come to the Lord's Mountain.** Add a sign that says, **God is with me here.** Place a cross and a picture of Jesus in the center. Add pictures from magazines or photographs of mountains. Display books about mountains and place storage containers with the necessary supplies for the activities around the center. Include beanbag chairs and large pillows for seats.

ACTIVITIES

WHAT ABOUT ZION?

Use your Bible, a Bible dictionary, and a Bible commentary to find out more about Zion.
- What does the word *Zion* mean?
- Where is the hill called Zion located? (*Hint:* It's mentioned in the Old Testament.)

God is with me here!

- What new name did an Old Testament king give to Zion?

- Zion isn't just a location. It's also a name for God's kingdom (see Psalm 76:2; Joel 3:16; Romans 11:26). It's a name that helps us remember something about God's love and protection, His promises, and the ways we worship Him. List the ways Zion means more than just a name of a mountain.

- Zion also is another name for our heavenly home with God. Read Hebrews 12:22–24; Revelation 14:1; 21:1–22:6. These Bible verses tell us what our life with Jesus in heaven will be like. Draw a picture or write a paragraph that describes how God and Zion are part of your life. Draw another picture or write another paragraph that tells what heaven will be like. Include images mentioned in the Bible verses.

GOD FROM A TO Z

```
GOD
Always loves me     N
B                   O
C                   P
D                   Q
E                   Redeemed me!
F                   Sends His angels
Gives               T
H                   U
I                   V
J                   Wants my prayers
K                   X
L                   Y
M                   Z
```

Write the alphabet from A to Z on a sheet of poster board or a large sheet of butcher paper. Draw a picture or write words or phrases that describe God's promises, actions, and plan for all believers that begin with each letter of the alphabet. Use a dictionary to help you think of words. Use the list as a prayer starter to thank God for everything from A to Z.

MAKE YOUR OWN ZION

In Bible times, everyone knew about Zion and the hill in Jerusalem where the temple was built. The Israelites said, "Let's go up to Zion!" or "We look for help from Zion!" They meant they were going to the temple or they were looking for help from God.

Where is your Zion? Maybe Zion is your church building. Maybe it's a place outside or inside where you sit and pray and think about God. Think of somewhere you can pray, praise, and worship God, either by yourself or with other believers. Make a cross to put in your Zion. Glue pieces of cardboard or wood together in a cross shape. Let dry. Glue nature objects such as seeds, seashells, dried flowers, pebbles, grasses, leaves, or small twigs to the cross. Let dry. Stand your cross in a lump of clay.

Put your cross in your Zion as a reminder of Jesus' death and resurrection for you. Add a Bible and a tape player with praise cassettes to your worship area. You also might include a list of prayer requests or prayer starters as a reminder to talk to God always.

MOUNTAINTOP WORSHIP BANNER

Work together to make a worship banner to display as a reminder that Jesus is always with you. Use an old window shade or a plain vinyl tablecloth as the background. Cut pictures from magazines and attach them to the background. Or draw or paint pictures on the background. Use marking pens to add words to the banner. Themes you might use include "God Is So Good," "Jesus Is Our King," or "Gifts from God." When finished, wrap the top 3" around a dowel rod or a 1" × 1" piece of lumber. Tie a heavy cord at either end of the rod as a hanger.

ZION ROCK

Use acrylic paint or permanent marking pens to add Christian symbols or favorite Bible verses to a clean, dry rock. Some phrases to use include: "Jesus is my Rock!" "God meets me at His mountain!" or "Jesus loves me." Make a Zion rock to give to friends and family members as a reminder that Jesus is with them always. Keep a pebble in your pocket to remind you of Jesus Christ, your Rock and Salvation.

PLASTER-OF-PARIS ROCKS, HILLS, AND MOUNTAINS

To the teacher: To prepare for this activity, cover the work area with a vinyl table-cloth or layers of newspaper. Mix plaster of paris according to directions.

Pour the plaster of paris mixture into a sturdy plastic bag and hold it closed. Squeeze the plaster to make a mountain, hills, or a rock formation. Hold the plaster in place until it begins to harden. When it has set, remove it from the bag. Use marking pens or acrylic paint to decorate the sculpture. Write **Jesus Is My Rock** on the sculpture. Cut a piece of felt to fit the bottom of your sculpture. Glue it in place. Display your mountain as a reminder of Jesus' strength.

CRYSTAL "HILLS" GARDEN

To the teacher: This experiment requires adult supervision. It involves chemicals (ammonia) and liquid bluing.

Place six or eight charcoal briquets in an aluminum pan. Pour ¼ cup each of salt, bluing, and ammonia into a coffee can or jar. Mix them together. Put different colors of food coloring on the briquets. Pour the salt mixture evenly over the briquets and place the pan in a warm place. The crystals will grow and make "hills." Mix more of the solution and keep it in a tightly closed jar. Add the solution to the crystal garden every two days to keep it growing.

BUILD A ZION PLACE

Use paper clips (or a stapler or tape) to connect paper cups. Work with your friends to stack layers of cups to build a mountain as high as possible. Or build a Zion place with building blocks. Make a sign for your mountain that says **Zion.** Share with a friend why Zion is a special name and place.

MOUNTAINS, HILLS, VALLEYS

Play this game in a gym or outside. Name one end of the playing area "Mountains," the middle area "Hills," and the opposite end "Valleys." The leader calls one of the locations, and everyone runs to get there. (You can play the game so everyone wins or eliminate the last two people who arrive at the location each time.)

MY FRIEND WENT WITH ME TO ZION

Gather several friends together for this game. Sit in a circle. Begin by saying, "My friend went with me to Zion, and she took a *(name something that begins with the first letter in the name of the person to your right).*" The person to your right repeats the first item and adds one that begins with the first letter of the next person's name. Continue until everyone has a turn. *Variation:* Name objects beginning with the letters of the alphabet from A to Z.

ALTAR CLOTH

Make an altar cloth for your classroom altar. Use a piece of fabric that covers the altar. Use fabric paint to draw Christian symbols or Bible verses on the cloth. Ask everyone to dip a hand in tempera paint and add his or her handprint. God's kingdom—Zion—is where believers gather together in Jesus' name!

MOVING MOUTH PUPPET

TANGRAM PUZZLE

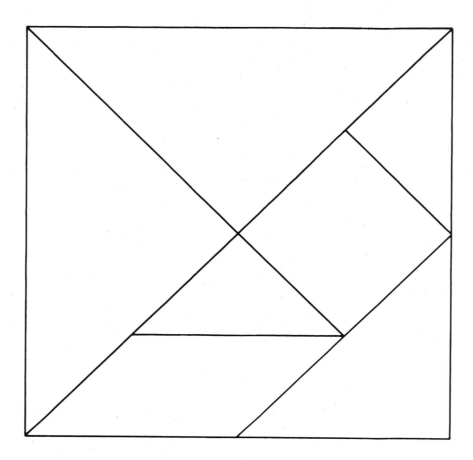

Can you use the tangram puzzle pieces to make these shapes?

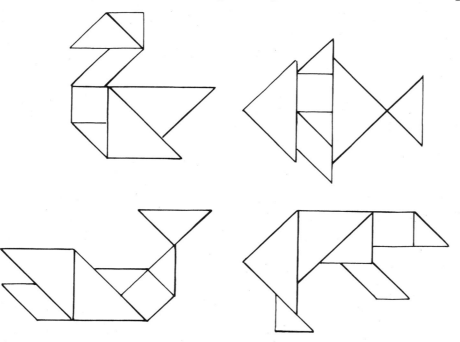

ORNAMENT SHAPES

Ornament Shapes